Documentary Research in Education, History and the Social Sciences

Documentary sources have become increasingly neglected in education and the social sciences, while historians use them but often take them for granted. This book seeks to emphasise their potential value and importance for an understanding of modern societies, while also recognising their limitations, and explores their relationship with other research strategies.

This up-to-date examination of how to research and utilise documents analyses texts from the past and present, considering sources ranging from personal archives to online documents and including books, reports, official documents and printed media.

This comprehensive analysis of the use of documents in research includes sections covering:

- Analysing documents
- Legal frameworks and ethical issues
- Records and archives
- Printed media and literature
- Diaries, letters and autobiographies

Documentary Research covers everything you need to know to make effective use of this important research technique and will be a valuable resource for all students, researchers and academics carrying out extensive research, particularly in the areas of education, history and the social sciences.

Gary McCulloch is Brian Simon Professor of History of Education at the Institute of Education, University of London.

Social Research and Educational Studies Series

Documentary Research in Education, History and the Social Sciences

Gary McCulloch

 Routledge
Taylor & Francis Group

LONDON AND NEW YORK

First published 2004 by Routledge
2 Park Square, Milton Park, Abingdon, Oxon, OX14 4RN

Simultaneously published in the USA and Canada
by Routledge
270 Madison Ave, New York NY 10016

Routledge is an imprint of the Taylor & Francis Group

Transferred to Digital Printing 2007

© 2004 Gary McCulloch

Typeset in Times by
BC Typesetting Ltd, Bristol

British Library Cataloguing in Publication Data
A catalogue record for this book is available from the British Library

Library of Congress Cataloging in Publication Data
McCulloch, Gary.
    Documentary research in education, history, and the social sciences
/ Gary McCulloch.
      – 1st ed.
        p.   cm. – (Social research and educational studies series; 22)
    Includes bibliographical references and index.
    ISBN 0–415–27286–6 (hardback: alk. paper) – ISBN 0–415–27287–4
(paperback: alk. paper)
      1. Social sciences–Research–Methodology. 2. Social sciences–
Archival resources. 3. Education–Research–Methodology.
    4. Education–Archival resources. 5. History–Research–Methodology.
    6. History–Sources. I. Title. II. Series.
      H62.M3336 2004
      300′.72–dc22   2003027012

ISBN 0–415–27286–6 (hbk)
ISBN 0–415–27287–4 (pbk)

Publisher's Note
The publisher has gone to great lengths to ensure the quality of this reprint
but points out that some imperfections in the original may be apparent

Contents

Case Studies

Series Editor's Preface

The purpose of the *Social Research and Educational Studies* series is to provide authoritative guides to key issues in educational research. The series includes overviews of fields, guidance on good practice and discussions of the practical implications of social and educational research. In particular, the series deals with a variety of approaches to conducting social and educational research. Contributors to the series review recent work, raise critical concerns that are particular to the field of education and reflect on the implications of research for educational policy and practice.

Each volume in the series draws on material that will be relevant for an international audience. The contributors to this series all have wide experience of teaching, conducting and using educational research. The volumes are written so that they will appeal to a wide audience of students, teachers and researchers. Altogether the volumes in the *Social Research and Educational Studies* series provide a comprehensive guide for anyone concerned with contemporary educational research.

The series includes individually authored books and edited volumes on a range of themes in education including qualitative research, survey research, the interpretation of data, self-evaluation, research and social policy, analysing data, action research and the politics and ethics of research.

A major gap in the methodological literature in education, history and the social sciences is a detailed treatment of documentary materials written by a researcher who has extensive experience in this field. Gary McCulloch's volume closes the gap through his analysis of methodological issues associated with documentary evidence. His focus is upon written documents that are produced in the course of everyday life rather than those specially commissioned by researchers. His book will be of value to a wide range of researchers working with documentary evidence, who will be able to draw on his experience in this authoritative work.

Robert G. Burgess
University of Leicester

Preface and Acknowledgements

This book draws on over twenty years of research experience based mainly on documentary sources of different types, involving first a doctorate in modern political history, and subsequently research in the history of education and on contemporary policy issues. It is also based on my experience of teaching research methods at undergraduate, Master's and doctoral levels, and from many discussions with students whose research I have supervised. Third, I have tried to learn from my professional experiences in Britain and New Zealand, as well as from a range of international literature that I have encountered during this time.

Some of the material in this work draws on externally funded research projects in which I have been involved. These are an Economic and Social Research Council project on professional cultures of teachers and the secondary school curriculum (000234738), and Leverhulme Trust projects on 'Education and the working class' (F/118/AB) and 'The life and educational career of Sir Cyril Norwood (1875–1956)' (F/118/AU).

I should like to thank copyright holders for kindly giving permission to reproduce material currently under copyright for the purposes of this book. May I also take this opportunity to give my sincere apologies to anyone whom I have not been able to contact.

This is also a suitable opportunity to thank the many librarians and archivists in different institutions who have enabled me to carry on my research, in particular those at the University of Sheffield, the Institute of Education London, the University of Leeds, the University of Cambridge, Lancaster University, the National Archive in London, the Modern Records Centre at the University of Warwick, and National Archives in Wellington and Auckland, New Zealand. Also in particular may I record my thanks to Sarah Canning and the late Ela Canning for their support for the Norwood project, and also Lawrence Morton, principal of Wales High School, Rotherham, for allowing me access to material held at his school.

All of my colleagues and students over the years will I hope recognise something of their own contribution to this book, and again I should like to emphasise my appreciation for this. Tom O'Donoghue, Pat Sikes and Jerry Wellington have read chapters of this work and discussed them with me, alerting me to a number of important issues which I greatly appreciate. All errors of fact and interpretation are mine alone.

RoutledgeFalmer have been very supportive of this project, and I should like to thank Anna Clarkson and also the series editor, Professor Robert Burgess, for their help and encouragement. Finally, I must single out my wife Sarah and my son Edward for their love and support, which I can only partially repay by dedicating this work to them both.

Gary McCulloch

1 Introduction: Reading between the Lines

The aim of this book is to discuss the role of documents of different kinds in the study of education, history and the social sciences. I hope to explore their established uses and limitations, and also to examine some of the new possibilities that are opening up in documentary-based studies of education and society. Documents are literally all around us, they are inescapable, they are an integral part of our daily lives and our public concerns. In our personal, private dealings, documents are basic and indispensable requirements. As Plummer notes, the world is crammed full of human, personal documents: 'People keep diaries, send letters, make quilts, take photos, dash off memos, compose auto/biographies, construct web sites, scrawl graffiti, publish their memoirs, write letters, compose CVs, leave suicide notes, film video diaries, inscribe memorials on tombstones, shoot films, paint pictures, make tapes and try to record their personal dreams' (Plummer 2001, p. 17).

At a public level, too, our identities are defined by the documents that are kept about us – documents such as birth certificates, examination results, driving licences, bank statements, newspaper stories, committee minutes, obituaries and wills. A key distinction can be made between private *documents*, on the one hand, and public *records*, on the other (see for example Hodder 1998). In this book I am considering both private documents and public records, in this sense, as 'documents' on which to base documentary studies. Constantly struck as I am by the ubiquity and convenience of the document, I wish therefore to proselytise, to evoke something of the potential power of documentary studies in education, history and the social sciences. To understand documents is to read between the lines of our material world. We need to comprehend the words themselves to follow the plot, the basic storyline. But we need to get between the lines, to analyse their meaning and their deeper purpose, to develop a study that is based on documents.

There are several further aspects of the present work that I need to explain before proceeding. First, it is mainly about *written* documents. Within this category I include such items as policy reports, committee papers, public treatises, works of fiction, diaries, autobiographies, newspapers, magazines and letters. Until very recently such artefacts were generally written on paper, whether by hand or mechanically. Over the past decade this has changed dramatically with the development of the World Wide Web. So it is vitally important now to take due account of electronic documents, including electronic mail and the data stored and communicated through the Internet. This major innovation has already helped to transform the nature of documentary studies and to extend its potential, and this process is likely to continue and to increase in its significance. On the other hand it is also important to be aware of underlying historical continuities. The invention of the printing press with a movable print type, credited to Johann Gutenberg of Mainz in the mid fifteenth century, had massive implications for the development of what has been described as a 'print culture' (Briggs and Burke 2002; Chartier 1987). According to Chartier (1987, p. 1),

> After Gutenberg, all culture in movable societies can be held to be a culture of the printed word, since what movable type and the printing press produced was not reserved (as in China and Korea) for the administrative use of the ruler but penetrated the entire web of social relations, bore thoughts and brought pleasures and lodged in people's deepest self as well as claiming its place in the public scene.

Nevertheless, a hierarchy of genres and forms of documents was maintained that owed much to the period before the Gutenberg revolution,

> between the great folio volume, the 'shelf-book' of the universities and of serious study, which had to be propped up to be read, the humanist book, more manageable in its mid-sized format, which served for classical texts and new works of literature, and the portable book, the pocket book or the bedside book of many uses, religious and secular, and of a wider and less selective readership.
>
> (Chartier 1988, p. 2)

By the same token, the electronic communications revolution of our own time, while transformative in many respects, may well retain and incorporate key elements of the print culture that has developed and spread over the past five hundred years.

Further to this, the present book is concerned mainly with documents that have been produced without any direct involvement on the part of the researcher, produced for other purposes and often with different priorities from those of the researcher. There is another type of documents that is deliberately produced by researchers as data for their research. This latter type is actively solicited by the researcher, and involves an interaction between the researcher and the producer of the document. As we will see, historically there have been a number of leading documentary researchers who have developed this kind of approach. It is a basic part of life history research, for instance, in which the researcher engages with the respondent to develop their life history, perhaps through interview-conversations, or group work, or keeping a journal, diary or other personal writings (see Goodson and Sikes 2001, especially chapter 2). More generally, transcripts of interviews or completed questionnaires might be included as documents of this type, documents prepared or facilitated by the researcher. As the ethnomethodologist Harold Garfinkel pointed out in the 1960s, documentary method is involved 'on the many occasions of survey research when the researcher, in reviewing his interview notes or in editing the answers to a questionnaire, has to decide "what the respondent had in mind"' (Garfinkel 1967, p. 95). More recently, David Silverman has suggested that the act of transcribing an interview turns it into a written text, and so makes a distinction between this kind of data and material recorded without the intervention of a researcher (Silverman 2001, p. 119; see also Silverman 2000, p. 40). Electronic technology has great potential for promoting the use of solicited documents, because of the rapid interchange that it makes possible, for interviewing through the medium of electronic mail for example, or the use of text messages and other convenient devices. A satisfactory treatment of the issues that arise from such research could be the subject of a separate work.

Equally, I am not principally concerned in this book with *visual* sources, such as paintings and film, although I take the point that, as Fairclough (1995) puts it, texts in contemporary society are increasingly 'multi-semiotic'. That is, even printed texts whose primary form is language increasingly combine this with other forms such as photographs and diagrams. According to Fairclough, 'We can continue regarding the text as a primarily linguistic cultural artefact, but develop ways of analysing other semiotic forms which are co-present with language, and especially how different semiotic forms interact in the multisemiotic text' (Fairclough 1995, p. 4). I am happy to attempt this where it seems appropriate, but will avoid going too far into this territory. At the same time, I also intend not to discuss *remains*, as distinct from records, such as buildings, furniture, dinosaur bones and Roman coins. Again, this kind of artefact would demand detailed attention deserving of a separate treatise.

In more positive vein, there are a number of issues about the intended coverage of this book that also deserve preliminary explanation. It seeks to draw on *international* literature and to engage with issues that are recognisable, even if not precisely the same, in different countries around the world. In doing so, my examples will be mainly British but also include some from the English-speaking world, or, even more to the point, that part of the world that reads and writes English. Some aspects of documentary studies I would conceive as global in scale, while others are naturally and irresistibly localised. For example, there are general issues about types of documents such as letters and newspapers, and about collections of documents in libraries. On the other hand, documents need also to be interpreted in the light of specific factors involved in their production and context, such as personal, social, political and historical relationships.

In framing the present work, I have been conscious of the different traditions operating in relation to documentary studies in history and in the social sciences. For historians, documents have provided the staple source material and are basic to their work. Yet historians have not on the whole been active in proselytising documentary research, nor in promoting a wider understanding of the theoretical and methodological issues involved in their use. As John Tosh has recently observed, history students have in the past not generally been given formal instruction in the nature of their own discipline, which is an approach that leaves a great deal to chance. He continues that, above all, 'students need to be aware of the limits placed on historical knowledge by the character of the sources and the working methods of historians' (Tosh 2002, pp. xix–xx). Yet there is still very little on offer that explains and discusses the nature of documentary evidence in a systematic and sustained manner.

The issues involved in documentary research are rather different for social scientists. Over the past twenty years, at least, social scientists have largely neglected and ignored the use of documents in favour of methods in which they are actively involved in producing data for their own purposes. Interviews, questionnaires and direct observation have become the basic tools of social research, while documents are seen as of only marginal utility. In this respect, then, the purpose of this book is to show possible uses of documentary studies in a wide range of social research, and also some of the limitations and dangers to be avoided.

In pursuing this dual purpose, this book draws a number of examples from education, both contemporary and historical. Education is interesting and useful partly because of its role in incorporating and transmitting cultural heritages and traditions, that is, it forms a means to develop knowledge, understanding and values from one generation to the next. In these ways it is a key dimension of history, albeit one that does not always receive the attention it deserves (McCulloch and Richardson 2000). It is also a major feature of social and economic policy in modern societies, especially in the modern period in the form of national systems of schooling, universities and, most latterly, lifelong learning. Moreover, it is closely related to other social issues, involving for example youth, crime, religion and work, that are of interest to social scientists from a range of backgrounds. Education itself has close connections with a number of social scientific disciplines and traditions, such as sociology, social policy, anthropology, politics, psychology and law, and I will emphasise these interconnections in the chapters that follow.

There are very few works that examine in depth the role of documentary sources either in history or in social research. The most significant study of this type, John Scott's book *A Matter of Record*, was published as long ago as 1990 (Scott 1990). Scott was interested in the handling of documents in relation to specific problems in social and historical research. He defined a document as 'an artefact which has as its central feature an inscribed text' (Scott 1990, p. 5). He gave most attention to the use of administrative papers produced by governmental and private agencies, which he regarded as the 'single most important category of documentary sources used in social research' (Scott 1990, p. 59), although he also included a chapter on mass communication and a short chapter on personal documents of various kinds. In the current work, while also stressing the importance of administrative records, I will give more extended attention to personal documents such as diaries, letters and autobiographies. I will also discuss the use of works of fiction as a tool of social research, unlike Scott, who neglected this kind of source. The impact of the Internet is also a key theme of the present work, which reflects something of the way that research in this area has changed since the publication of Scott's work more than a decade ago.

Other recent works are also relevant to this present study but also have limitations as general appraisals of the role of documents in social research. Plummer's (2001), for example, is a classic analysis of personal documents, but does not attempt to investigate public or official documentation. Carolyn Steedman has produced a highly provocative study of archives, entitled simply *Dust* (2001), but contents herself with this particular realm of documents. Lindsay Prior's *Using Documents in Social Research* (2003) is a more general treatment, is interesting at a theoretical level and includes a number of useful examples of documents and their use. On the other hand it is not very accessible in its discussion of documents in action, and does not seek to develop a clear discussion of different types of documents, on the grounds that, as he argues, 'The active document is usually too slippery a creature to fall neatly into such classificatory traps' (Prior 2003, p. 28).

In my approach to the topic I should like also to give some consideration to the historical development of documentary studies in education, history and the social sciences. Very little has been written in this vein, although there are a number of interesting works on particular forms of documents and how these have developed over time. Plummer (2001, especially chapter 5) offers a useful discussion of the history of life history methods. Scott (1990) does not develop this kind of approach, even in relation to official records in which he is particularly interested. It is Gordon Allport's work, published in the 1940s, that is most helpful in beginning to appraise the historical growth of this area of study. To be sure, Allport (1947) was himself concerned mainly with psychological dimensions of personal documents. Nevertheless, his interpretation was of wider significance for social science method in general, and for the notion that he put forward of a continuing process of building on previous work of this type to develop a research tradition. Sixty years on, further assessment and review of this nature seems overdue.

A further point about my approach to this work is that I emphasise the need to try to understand documents in relation to their milieux, or in other words to relate the *text* to its *context*. It is necessary to find out as much as possible about the document from internal evidence elicited from the text itself, but it is no less important to discover how and why it was produced and how it was received. Documents are social and historical constructs, and to examine them without considering this simply misses the point. For the same reasons, documents need also to be understood with reference to their *author/s* and to what they were seeking to achieve, in so far as this can be known. I therefore do not wish to align this work with post-structuralist critiques such as that of Roland Barthes which focus so closely on the text and its readership – 'textuality' – that they tend to deny the significance of the author and claim that the meaning can never be known (Barthes 1977; see also for example Young 1981; Burke 1992). I am also very interested in the potential link between past and present, but hopefully not at the expense of becoming ahistorical or anachronistic in my approach to documents, which must be interpreted in relation to the historical context in which they are produced (see McCulloch and Richardson 2000).

This leads on in turn to a further explanatory point, which is about my own personal and professional background and how this informs my outlook on documentary studies. I was trained as a historian, and it is second nature for me to use documents to peer into the past. I have spent long days of toil over many years in this pursuit. In doing so I have used many different kinds of documents, official and personal, publicly available and under lock and key. Most of my own research has centred on nineteenth- and twentieth-century England, although I have also spent several years researching in New Zealand. My interests have focused increasingly on education – the history of education, especially, but also the ways in which this history relates to our contemporary policies and problems (see for example McCulloch 1998). In addressing historical issues in education, I have always been concerned to relate them to broader social issues, to cultivate a social history of education that would be of interest both to educationists and to historians (McCulloch 2000a). Economic, cultural, political, geographical and many other issues have also been prominent in this work. In linking the past to the present, I have been keen to find frameworks and ways of working through which to bring them closer together. The ways in which I work with documents illustrate, indeed they permeate, these concerns. Documents can provide potent evidence of continuity and change in ideals and in practices, in private and in the public arena. They are a significant medium through which to understand the way in which our society has developed, and how it continues to develop. Yet they also reflect a basic tension in our society, a rupture between its present and its past. Documentary studies need to come to terms with this alienation from history, and to find ways of reconciling the historical with the contemporary.

Lastly, I should emphasise that this book is not intended to be simply about 'method' in a technical sense, although I do hope that it may be useful for students and scholars in thinking through the ways in which they work with documents. It is more broadly about 'methodology', that is, it is concerned with why and when to use documents, and not just with how to use them. And, more deeply, it tries to relate theory and methodology in documentary studies. Tim May has rightly argued that 'The ways in which documents are used is clearly a methodological and theoretical question, as well as a matter for the technicalities that surround method' (May 2001, p. 177). He adds that different approaches to documents are 'fundamental to how we see our surroundings and ourselves' (May 2001, p. 178). I should like to pursue this key theme further in this present work.

In approaching documents in this way, as in much else, I am conscious of the advice offered by C. Wright Mills in his classic work, *The Sociological Imagination*. Mills was insistent that theory and method should not be considered separately, but should always be related to each other, and also to actual problems. As he argued,

> For the classic social scientist, neither method nor theory is an autonomous domain; methods are methods for some range of problems; theories are theories of some range of phenomena. They are like the language of the country you live in: it is nothing to brag about that you can speak it, but it is a disgrace and an inconvenience if you cannot.

> (Mills 1959, p. 121)

According to Mills, 'Controversy over different views of "methodology" and "theory" is properly carried on in close and continuous relation with substantive problems' (Mills 1959, p. 128). Grappling with these issues in this way was, for Mills, the best way to develop what he called 'intellectual craftsmanship'. The key issue with which Mills himself was concerned was the distinction between 'personal troubles', in which an individual finds his or her values being threatened, and 'public issues', involving crises in institutional arrangements. In a time of rapid and often threatening social change, it was the task of the 'sociological imagination' to relate personal troubles to public issues.

There are a number of key points relevant to the current work that emerge from Mills's analysis. The first concerns the nature of historical studies. Mills emphasises the close relationship between history and sociology, and indeed argues that history is the 'shank of social study' (Mills 1959, p. 143). Historians represent in his view 'the organised memory of mankind' (Mills 1959, p. 144), which sociologists need to recognise and tap by including a 'historical scope of conception and a full use of historical materials' (Mills 1959, p. 143). The challenge that Mills poses for historians, conversely, is to engage with theoretical and methodological issues more fully and explicitly than they have been wont to do. He perceives a wide range of theoretical and methodological issues in any work of history, which, he suggests, 'makes the calm unawareness of many historians all the more impressive'. Such unawareness, according to Mills, has become untenable:

> I suppose there have been periods in which perspectives were rigid and monolithic and in which historians could remain unaware of the themes taken for granted. But ours is not such a period; if historians have no 'theory', they may provide materials for the writing of history, but they cannot themselves write it. They can entertain, but they cannot keep the record straight. That task now requires explicit attention to much more than 'the facts'.
>
> (Mills 1959, p. 145)

This is a point that is also recognised and developed, much more recently, by the historian Richard Evans (1997). Mills therefore defines a twofold challenge, for social scientists to recognise the nature and importance of historical thinking and methods, and for historians to be more alert to the demands of theory and methodology. The current work is intended as a contribution in both of these directions, taking as its starting point the tasks involved in the use of documentary materials.

The second key issue that Mills identified is about the relationship between biography, history and social structures. The study of individual lives has often been developed in isolation from broader considerations of historical and social dimensions. Conversely, historical and social inquiry have been prone to ignore the personal and the individual in their emphasis on the bigger picture. Mills reminds us of the need to try to understand the relationship between the individual and the structural, as a key component of his ideal of the sociological imagination, which makes possible an understanding of 'the larger historical scene' in terms of 'its meaning for the inner life and the external career of a variety of individuals' (Mills 1959, p, 5). Indeed, he continues, 'The sociological imagination enables us to grasp history and biography and the relations between the two within society.' This was, he contends, a prime concern of the classic social analysts: 'No social study that does not come back to the problems of biography, of history, and of their intersections within a society has completed its intellectual journey' (Mills 1959, p. 6). Thus, according to Mills, a key issue both for historians and for social scientists is to develop the capacity 'to range from the most impersonal and remote transformations to the most intimate features of the human self – and to see the relations between the two' (Mills 1959, p. 7). The interaction between 'personal troubles' and 'public issues' is here at its most explicit. This book will seek ways of highlighting such connections through documentary study.

This interaction also raises a further set of considerations around the nature of the 'public' and the 'private' in modern societies. Jürgen Habermas has proposed that the 'public sphere', or *Öffentlichkeit*, based on public people coming together as a public, became increasingly dissociated from the 'intimate sphere' of private family relations during the eighteenth century. The family became increasingly 'private', he suggests, while the world of work and organisation became ever more 'public' (Habermas 1992). There have been a number of critiques of Habermas's work (Calhoun 1992). In particular, it has been noted that the dimension of gender relations, absent from his study, is an important aspect of the polarisation between the private and the public, in which women became increasingly confined during the nineteenth century to the domestic sphere of the family, while men directed themselves towards the public realm (see for example Eley 1992). Moreover, as Habermas himself pointed out, the private and the public have often engaged in 'mutual infiltration' and 'reciprocal permeation' (Habermas 1992, pp. 145, 151). The current work will seek to take account of these social-historical issues around the development of modern societies. Documentary studies have tended to follow the basic divisions between the private and the public, especially in terms of the separation between 'personal documents' as examined by Burgess (1984a) and Plummer (2001), and 'public records' discussed by Scott (1990). While recognising the differences in emphasis and orientation involved in these distinctions, the present book will seek to highlight the infiltrations and permeations between the two spheres. For example, sources that are normally seen as personal documents can shed light on public issues, while public records may be very helpful towards a greater understanding of even the most personal, intimate and everyday concerns of ordinary people.

The structure of the book is designed to facilitate these aims. I begin with a historical discussion of social research and its use of documents. This is followed in Chapter 3 by an overview of issues involved in doing documentary research. Chapter 4 considers archives and records, Chapter 5 printed media and literature, and Chapter 6 diaries, letters and autobiographies. Although these different types of documents are thus demarcated, I hope to show how their uses can be interrelated, and also how researchers can combine them in their work. The final chapter adds some further brief comments to elaborate on the connections between these documentary sources, and also between documents and other kinds of sources and methods.

Introduction

Following each chapter, I will make some suggestions for further reading, both of more detailed discussions of particular aspects that are addressed in the chapter and of examples of documents that could be studied at first hand. I also include a number of extended case studies of documents of different types to facilitate direct analysis and discussion of these, while more generally I have tried to provide extensive examples of documentary evidence in different contexts.

Overall, therefore, my investigation of the uses of documents in the chapters that follow will seek to understand and address two key problems which I have encountered in my own work, and which are also pressing issues in education, history, and the social sciences more generally. These are, first, the relationship between past and present, and, secondly, the tensions and interactions between public and private. I will be looking for ways in which documents can be used to bring together the past and the present, the public and the private. I will be seeking to read between the lines of documentary sources, in order to help enhance our understanding of education, history and modern societies. Before I move forward in these directions, however, there is a prior task. Documents have themselves become unfashionable as tools or resources in educational and social research. They may be familiar, they are often convenient and they can even be inexpensive, but they are also unpopular. It is important to try to understand why this is so, in order to make the fullest use of them. Somehow, we have become alienated from them. So there is a paradox here that I would like to explore more fully before beginning to explore their potential in any depth. How can they be so familiar, and yet so strange?

Suggestions for further reading

Burgess, R. (1984) *In the Field: An Introduction to Field Research*, Routledge, London

McCulloch, G. and Richardson, W. (2000) *Historical Research in Educational Settings*, Open University Press, Buckingham

May, T. (2001) *Social Research: Issues, Methods and Process*, 3rd edn, Open University Press, Buckingham

Mills, C. Wright (1959) *The Sociological Imagination*, Oxford University Press, London

Plummer, K. (2001) *Documents of Life 2: An Invitation to a Critical Humanism*, Sage, London

Prior, K. (2003) *Using Documents in Social Research*, Sage, London

Scott, J. (1990) *A Matter of Record*, Polity, Cambridge

2 Paper Tigers

Social Research and Documentary Studies

It was the Chinese leader Mao Tse-tung who popularised the phrase 'paper tiger' when pointing out the underlying weakness of the United States that belied its apparent strength. Such an epithet might be appropriate in describing the exponents of documents themselves, who could draw on abundant resources but failed to demonstrate their power. In this chapter we will examine the development of social research over the past century, the attempts that were made to promote the use of documents and a general decline in their use over the past half-century.

A number of commentators in recent years have noted a distinct lack of interest in the use of documents in educational and social research. This has been reflected partly in the scarcity of documentary-based studies, and also in the scant attention given to documents in most social research methods texts. Jennifer Platt complained in the early 1980s that discussions of the use of documents in the standard methodological literature were 'sparse and patchy' (Platt 1981, p. 31). This was to become a common refrain. Robert Burgess argued that the lack of systematic accounts of documentary evidence in 'methods' textbooks amounted to a 'major omission' (Burgess 1984a, p. 123). More recently, Tim May has conceded that 'the volume of writings devoted to this topic is not so great' (May 2001, p. 176). According to Lindsay Prior, too, 'For those students who wish to centre their work on the study of documents – or, even, to take account of documents in their research work – there are very few pronouncements on methodology available' (Prior 2003, p. ix). This lacuna is exemplified in a lengthy work edited by Dawn Burton, *Research Training for Social Scientists* (2000a), 'deliberately wide ranging in its coverage and specifically designed as a one-stop text' (p. xiv), that finds no room for most kinds of documentary methods.

This was not always the case. In the first half of the twentieth century, there were many important works of educational and social research that were based exclusively or partly on documentary sources, and also several useful methodological discussions about the uses and limitations of such sources. Moreover, such works shed light on both historical and contemporary dimensions of education and society, and on the relationship between private and public concerns. In this chapter therefore I will first of all review some of this earlier literature in the field, and then seek to explain the decline of this general approach that has taken place over the past fifty years.

Documents and social life

In the early decades of the twentieth century, the emerging social sciences were faced with the challenge of coming to terms with the nature of mass society, including such major developments as the spread of urbanisation and industrialisation, the growth of social institutions such as schools and hospitals, and the encroaching power of the State. At the same time, they needed to understand the position of individuals in the face of these massive changes. In addressing these issues, the favoured methods of nineteenth-century social scientists, especially the statistical survey and the general theories of 'armchair sociologists', seemed increasingly inadequate for the task. What seemed to be required were new ways of comprehending both people and the wider configurations around them. There was strong potential in doing so from current insights in the social sciences. New developments in psychology had made significant advances into the human mind, although these tended to emphasise individual rather than social factors. It was necessary to develop the connections between the personal and the social in order to make further headway in the study of social development. In anthropology, too, there was significant progress, but this was applied to primitive rather than modern cultures, and there needed to be some way of relating the methods and perspectives involved in this to the metropolitan communities of the twentieth century.

As they pondered these problems, many sociologists discovered that significant clues lay all around them. If modern civilisation was built in bricks and metal, and fuelled by coal and oil, it was inscribed on paper. The bureaucracies of the nation-states produced copious records of their development, and of their dealings with different interest groups. They produced large numbers of reports on the problems that they encountered and the policies that they favoured, and their consultations were also transcribed in loving detail. The new social institutions also kept details of decisions made and of their burgeoning staff and clienteles. Strict, formal record keeping was routinised and became a discipline in its own right. Such records might well provide insights into the processes and workings of the social structures of the modern age.

These developments took place at a time when communications were being transformed. New systems of transport became widely established in the nineteenth century, with the railways at the forefront. The train was especially important as a means of distribution. It helped to make possible the rise of mass-circulation newpapers, and it also allowed individuals to send personal messages as letters over short and long distances relatively quickly. In the year 1920, over five thousand million letters, postcards and packets were posted in the United Kingdom alone, amounting to about four items per week for each adult, and the traffic in mail borne by the transport system continued to rise thereafter (Clarke 1996, p. 113). The daily newspaper was a major social and political influence, together with more specialist magazines which were produced less frequently, but could focus on particular themes of the day in greater detail. The reading public was bombarded with journalism and commentary to suit every taste. Increasingly cheap book production, buttressed by the rise of paperbacks in the interwar years, also encouraged the mass circulation of fiction and non-fiction in book format.

By the same token, many individuals who were caught up in these contemporary changes took it upon themselves to record their own reactions and responses, sometimes for the benefit of themselves and their families, sometimes for a wider audience. Literacy was widespread by the end of the nineteenth century, and so was the urge to leave a mark to explain the successes and failures of a lifetime. Diary writing became fashionable among the middle classes, and autobiographies were not uncommon. Hence, just as the modern state and the agencies and institutions of the modern world transcribed themselves on paper, so there was a parallel development in which individuals became accustomed to writing themselves into the script. Such documents, public and personal, constituted a potentially massive resource for social researchers.

The literature of the 1920s and 1930s provides some key examples of the increasing use of documents in educational and social research. The basic concern of these works was to reveal the nature of the social life of particular communities in a number of specific contexts. Documents were central to this kind of examination, whether the study was based entirely on documentary sources of different kinds, or whether it employed them in concert with a range of other kinds of source material. In the United States, such studies were strongly encouraged by the so-called Chicago school of sociology, based at the Department of Sociology at the University of Chicago, founded in 1892 and at the peak of its influence from the First World War until the mid-1930s (Coser 1979).

The benchmark text of documentary-based studies of this time was *The Polish Peasant in Europe and America*, by William I. Thomas and Florian Znaniecki (1918–20/1927). This major work, originally published in five volumes, set out to trace the effects of emigration to the United States on the Polish community. It explored the challenges that such emigration posed to the settled social values of Polish peasants, and the extent of the disintegration that resulted. In doing so, it tried to systematise and classify the attitudes and values that prevailed in this specific social group. Thomas and Znaniecki explicitly based their work on what they described as 'concrete materials' (1918–20/1927, vol. 1, p. 76), both solicited for the purposes of their research and unsolicited. In the early part of the study they made use of personal letters to or from emigrants, providing extensive quotation from 764 such letters. The middle section of the work drew on newspapers and institutional records. These, as the authors commented, were of a 'much less direct and personal character' than the letters used earlier, and tended also to be less 'naïve and unreflective' (vol. 2, pp. 1122–3). The records of the Juvenile Court, for example, were used to provide copious evidence of delinquency (of boys) and sexual immorality (of girls). Lastly, they made use of the life-record of an immigrant. This comprised a 312-page autobiography, written at their request, by a Polish immigrant named Wladek Wiszniuewski, to exemplify the disorganising effect on an individual of the passage from an old to a new form of social organisation. Their study as a whole sought to explain contemporary social problems through an understanding of the past, including the past lives of immigrants, the general social organisation of the Polish community, and the traditions and social ideals that they had inherited. In the pursuit of this overarching issue, documents were highly revealing and evocative.

Thomas and Znaniecki were especially enthusiastic about the potential for the life-record document. As they explained,

> We are safe in saying that personal life-records, as complete as possible, constitute the *perfect* type of sociological material, and that if social science has to use other materials at all it is only because of the practical difficulty of obtaining at the moment a sufficient number of such records to cover the totality of sociological problems, and of the enormous amount of work demanded for an analysis of all the personal materials necessary to characterize the life of a social group.
>
> (vol. 2, pp. 1832–3)

Indeed, they added, 'If we are forced to use mass-phenomena as material, or any kind of happenings taken without regard to the life-histories of the individuals who participate in them, it is a defect, not an advantage, of our present sociological method' (vol. 2, p. 1833). They also insisted that such life-records, while inherently personal and individual, would be valuable tools of social research. Unlike bureaucratic records, they could 'reach the actual human experiences and attitudes which constitute the full, live and active social reality behind the formal organization of social institutions' (vol. 2, p. 1834). Moreover, they were superior to statistical data, 'which taken in themselves are nothing but symptoms of unknown causal processes and can serve only as provisional ground for sociological hypotheses' (vol. 2, p. 1834). In order to achieve their full potential, Thomas and Znaniecki argued, such life-records needed to be limited to representative cases of social types, which meant developing what they envisaged as a theory of human individuals as social personalities (vol. 2, p. 1835). Thus, their work sought to relate the private, personal, intimate concerns of individuals to the collective, public, social realm through the use of a broad range of documentary materials.

Case Study 1
The Polish Peasant

Thomas and Znaniecki's *The Polish Peasant in Europe and America* draws on a rich and diverse range of documentary sources to illustrate the social and cultural disintegration of Polish immigrants in the United States in the early part of the twentieth century. Here is a selection of these sources, taken from the 1927 edition. They are interesting for what they say about individual, concrete experiences; for their significance in relating historical traditions to contemporary changes; and for their implications in linking private troubles to public issues.

Letter 571 – Borkowski series, vol. 1, p. 891

[*The husband emigrated to America in 1893, leaving his wife behind in Poland. There she lived in increasing penury and isolation until her death, apparently some twenty years later. The following letter is drawn from a sequence of letters, with an accompanying commentary, volume 1, pp. 869–900.*]

August 6, 1910
DEAR HUSBAND: I write to you with great timidity, but despair obliges me to write so openly. I beg you, dear Wladek, I beg you for God's sake, have pity and send me a little money, for I can find no way out. I tried to get from the Philanthropic Association at least a few tickets for a few pounds of bread and a few pints of gruel monthly, but they refused me, for they learned that I have a husband. They say that it is for them all the same whether this husband is in Warsaw or in America, but I have a husband. So I don't know what to do with myself. I have no work, for now even a poor servant maid wants [her dresses] to be sewn on a machine with different adornments, for such is the fashion. And, to tell the truth, I begin to lose my eyes with sewing and crying. So I only implore first our Lord God, then you for mercy upon me. Have pity, dear husband, send me [money] as soon as possible, because I owe for rent, I owe to Sliwinska, and I have no

continued on next page

---

possibility of paying them, while every day I must nourish myself, and I have nothing. Although I economize every grosz from you and nourish myself with anything in order only to live through the day, yet everything is so expensive, particularly rent. I live in a basement, my bed in a corner, a box and a small table before the bed, and I pay for it 3 roubles and 2 zloty [3 roubles, 30] a month, and they hardly permit me sometimes to cook a little with my own fuel, and so it is everywhere . . .

TEOFILA BORKOWSKA

Dear husband, write me whether you will come some day to Warsaw? It is true that you have put aside some money, but on the other hand you are far away from your family and from your land. And after so many years you would have had better conditions even here, and more than one pain would be spared to you. For it seems to me that sometimes it is not very pleasant for you there, and more than once perhaps you long for your people. Write me, dear Wladek; let me at least have some illusion that I shall still see you.

Newspaper extract 22 – vol. 2, p. 1176

The old folks dress modestly in this locality but the same cannot be said of the youth. It is pitiful to see so many girls who as soon as they see a stylish skirt or jacket or bobbed hair worn, by one of the worst kind perhaps, want to dress accordingly, but do not realise that it is shameful and disgraceful for the village youth. There are, I dare say, some good-for-nothing boys who, having donned a pretty, nice looking overcoat or a stylish suit of clothes and shoes, not only would not salute reverently one who wears a peasant's coat, but would not even stop to converse with him. Every one of these profligate boys reflects thus: 'I dress better than that one does, I may possess a bigger fortune; then why should I speak to him.' Should you visit his home, however, you would never suppose that such a dressy young man lives there, for the house is filled thick with dirt and filth. Such was not the state of affairs in Ostrow years ago. Therefore it is not to be wondered at that Roch Soczewka, during his stay here several years ago, did not find any elegance and reported to the Gazeta that all the inhabitants of Ostrow dress modestly. Today nearly one-half of the girls dress above their means and there are also several who are not worthy of mention.
Gazeta Swiatezna, 1893, 5.

continued on facing page

Public records 58 – vol. 2, p. 1719

Koskowski Family. Pauline Klimek came to America when she was 16 years old. She was doing housework in Philadelphia when she met Felix Koskowski and was induced to live with him as his wife. She claimed that she did not then know that he had a wife who had returned to her home in Austrian Poland for her confinement. When the newly born child was 14 months old, Mrs Koskowski returned to the United States. She found her husband in Chicago living with Pauline Klimek. She appealed to the Polish National Alliance for help. Koskowski and Pauline were arrested on an adultery charge but when the judge found that Pauline was pregnant he took pity on her and agreed to dismiss the case if she would have Koskowski arrested on a bastardy charge. He did not make any context, but this suit was also dismissed, for it appeared that Koskowski had no money to pay a judgement, if he were sent to the House of Correction his wife and child would suffer, and moreover Pauline had no hard feelings against him and did not want him to be sent to jail. The Immigrants' Protective Association found work for Pauline and planned to befriend her through her confinement. However, without any notice, she left the place where she was working and ran away once more with Koskowski. Mrs Koskowski and the child were left in Chicago without any means of support.

From the *Records of the Chicago Legal Aid Society*.

Life record of an immigrant, extract, vol. 2, p. 1918

I begin my description with the first day that I went to school. I was exactly six years old when my father took me by the hand and led me to the school, a few yards distant from our house. When the teacher learned what brought us to him he gave me a look and my examination began. Here I must mention that I knew already all the Polish and Russian letters well, for my older brothers and sisters had taught them to me at home. The teacher gave me a book, first a Polish, then a Russian one; I knew how to read well, so he patted my head and told me to sit down on the first, that is, preparatory bench. I sat down and began to look around the class-room. The teacher spoke for a while with my father, then they separated, and my studies began. At ten o'clock on the same day, during recess, some boys came to me and gave me a few knocks, which made me cry. When the teacher came I was still crying. He asked me what was the matter. I answered,

continued on next page

> half-crying, that the boys had beaten me. He laughed, patted me again on the head and said that it would not happen again. And it was true; they did not laugh at me, nor beat me any more. This made me bolder and gave me courage to learn. And so one day after another passed. The teacher was still a young man, and as he had only an old mother living with him, he came often enough to visit us. As he knew me well he treated me tolerably. My brother Stanislaw helped me. He had been going to school for two years and learned very well; the teacher praised him, and my father promised him that he should be a priest if he continued to study well. Stanislaw and I loved each other, so I never had any difficulty with my lessons. School began in November and ended in April, and the rest of the year was vacation. Then there was a merry life! Sometimes I went fishing with a hook, sometimes to the forest in search of birds, or to pick mushrooms or berries. In a word, I was free.

It is also notable that *The Polish Peasant in Europe and America* attracted a great deal of methodological attention. One influential discussion, by Herbert Blumer, was especially interesting for the way in which it challenged the representativeness, the adequacy, the reliability and the validity of the interpretation of the documents used by Thomas and Znaniecki, especially the extensive use of personal letters. Blumer complained that with regard to representativeness, it was unclear how the authors collected these letters, and how they had made their selections. So far as adequacy was concerned, information was lacking about the life, setting and background of the individuals involved. He questioned the reliability of the experiences that were recounted as it was not possible to test the honesty or truthfulness of the accounts. He was also unconvinced by the interpretation of these documents, and critical of the lack of criteria to support the authors' interpretation (Blumer 1939, pp. 36–7). Nevertheless, as Blumer acknowledged at a major conference held in New York at the end of 1938, *The Polish Peasant* had been widely influential:

> the work of Thomas and Znaniecki has exerted a tremendous amount of influence among sociologists and has given rise to the rather vigorous prosecution of research involving the use of human documents, especially of life records and life histories. This has become a standard, but not a standardised, method in sociological and socio-psychological research.
>
> (Blumer 1939, pp. 129–30)

In particular, according to Blumer, this work had encouraged sociologists to overcome a dependence on 'armchair' theorising in favour of 'concrete, empirical investigations which employ large masses of data which can be used by subsequent investigators' (Blumer 1939, p. 192).

Subsequent discussions also emphasised the importance of using personal documents. Gordon Allport, for example, promoted their use in psychology to form a bond with other social sciences 'at the level of the concrete case' (Allport 1947, p. 47). Indeed, according to Allport, 'Raw documents have served as the sea upon which authentic scientific voyages of discovery have been launched' (Allport 1947, p. 176). Other commentators celebrated the use of personal documents in history, anthropology and sociology (for example Gottschalk, Kluckhohn and Angell 1947). Nevertheless, it was significant that the sociologist Robert Angell warned of the danger of social researchers moving away from one extreme of 'armchair sociology' towards the opposite extreme of 'wishing to deal only with what they believe to be cold, hard facts' (Angell 1947, p. 231). This 'objective' tendency in social science research was soon to overwhelm what Angell (1947, p. 226) described as the 'slow but steady', even if incomplete and 'not very impressive', development in the use of personal documents.

Several other notable documentary-based studies were produced in these years besides *The Polish Peasant*. One such was *Middletown*, by Robert and Helen Lynd (1929), which set out to provide a systematic observation of an American community and its activities by drawing on a wide range of techniques including a number of types of documentary material. The Lynds' work was strongly influenced by social anthropology in its minute examination of social and cultural interactions. The authors also attempted to establish a historical dimension in the study, by comparing the contemporary life of Middletown with the situation as it had existed in 1890, when industrial changes were beginning to transform the nature of the community.

Although a range of techniques including participation in local life, compilation of statistics, interviews and questionnaires were also employed, documentary material was fundamental to the Lynds' study. This involved examination of census data, city and county records, court files, school records, State Biennial Reports and Year Books. The two leading daily newspapers were read in detail for the years 1890 and 1891, supplemented by the daily paper associated with the Democratic Party and a labour paper. The current newspapers were studied systematically during the course of the study. Minutes of various organisations such as the Board of Education, the Missionary Societies of two leading churches, the Ministerial Association, the Federated Club of Clubs, the Women's Club, the Library Board and the Humane Society were studied for both the earlier and the current period and usually the intervening years. School examination papers were compared in detail over the period as a whole. Two detailed diaries, one of a leading merchant and prominent Protestant churchman and one of a young Catholic baker, were read for the years 1886 to 1900, together with other diaries, scrapbooks, programmes, letters and club papers, with the aim of providing an equivalent of the informal contacts of today. Local and regional histories, city directories, maps, Chamber of Commerce publications, high-school annuals and surveys of the city completed the trawl of relevant documentary sources (Lynd and Lynd 1929, pp. 506–7).

The way in which these sources were combined may be gleaned from the Lynds' treatment of changes in the nature of housing (Lynd and Lynd 1929, pp. 97–8):

> It is estimated that in 1890 only about one family in six or eight had even the crudest running water – a hydrant in the yard or a faucet at the iron kitchen sink. A leading citizen thought it sufficiently important to enter in his diary in 1890 that a neighbor 'has a hydrant for his house'. The minutes of the Board of Education for 1888 contain an item: 'Eph Smell . . . 1 wooden pump for high school . . . $10.00'. . . . According to the City Engineer, only two-thirds of the houses had sewer connections in 1924.

As elsewhere in their study, the Lynds are often vague in their referencing to particular sources. Nevertheless, in this passage it is apparent that they have drawn on several different types of documentary source to provide a comprehensive account of the development of housing in Middletown. In the process, it succeeds in shedding light on both historical and contemporary aspects of change and on the relationship between the past and the present. Indeed, it is highly sophisticated in its portrayal of uneven development, and the continuities and differences that underlay the process of change. Moreover, this treatment also has significant implications for the relationship between private concerns and public issues. The intimate details of personal hygiene and the personal possessions of individual consumers are directly connected to technological change, culture and class.

Similarly, in relation to school life, the Lynds noted the increasingly prominent role of the school in the life of children over the previous fifty years: 'Today the school is becoming not a place to which children go from their homes for a few hours daily but a place from which they go home to eat and sleep' (Lynd and Lynd 1929, p. 212). They compared the high-school annual of 1924 with the first annual, produced thirty years before, in order to demonstrate this perceived widening of the school's function. To some extent, they suggested (p. 212), change could be discerned from the percentage of space devoted to different topics in these respective works:

Next in importance to the pictures of the senior class and other class data in the earlier book, as measured by the percentage of space occupied, were the pages devoted to the faculty and the courses taught by them, while in the current book athletics shares the position of honor with the class data, and a faculty twelve times as large occupies relatively only half as much space. Interest in small selective group 'activities' has increased at the expense of earlier total class activities.

Yet, according to the Lynds, this kind of numerical comparison failed to convey a significant difference in tone between the two books: 'The description of academic work in the annual beginning, "Among the various changes that have been effected in grade work are . . ." and ending, "regular monthly teachers' meetings have been inaugurated", seems as foreign to the present high school as does the early class motto "Deo Duce"; equally far from 1890 is the present dedication, "To the Bearcats"' (Lynd and Lynd 1929, p. 212).

Wilfred Waller also investigated the social world of the school and of teachers by trying to understand the relationships of the people involved in concrete situations. This led him away from a dependence on statistical method, and towards the 'direct study of social phenomena' (Waller 1932/ 1967, preface). His analysis of these phenomena was primarily sociological, while the methods that he employed in gathering and interpreting material were empirical and observational. He also drew on a wide range of insights borrowed in some cases from anthropologists in their detailed descriptions of social behaviour, and in others from the materials of realistic novelists with their emphasis on inward human motivations. Waller expressed a strong preference for the use of personal documents such as life histories, case records, diaries and letters. Moreover, he declared, in interpreting these he would be guided by concepts developed across the social sciences including psychology, psychiatry and sociology, 'neither dragging any interpretation in by the heels nor failing to cross academic boundary lines in search of usable interpretations' (Waller 1932/1967, p. 2).

The major texts that were produced in this period to provide advice on how to develop research in the new social sciences were notable for their emphasis on the use of documents. The eminent sociologist Emile Durkheim, for instance, was insistent on documentary study as the key to social research, especially if the documents concerned could be not simply 'accumulated' but studied selectively and critically. According to Durkheim, the principal material for the inductions of the sociologist should be 'the societies whose beliefs, traditions, customs, and law have taken shape in written and authentic documents' (Durkheim 1938/1966, pp. 133–4). Ethnographic methods also had a part to play, he continued, but rather than being the main element in research they should only constitute 'a supplement to historical data', or should at least be confirmed by such data (Durkheim

1927/1950, p. 134). In the case of Durkheim, it also seems worth noting that his key research offered significant insights both into the relationship between past and present and into the connections between the private and the public realms. His work on secondary education adopted a historical approach to understand the nature of contemporary problems, arguing as he did that 'After all, what is history if it is not an analysis of the present, since the constituent components of the present are only to be found in the past?' (Durkheim 1938/1977, p. 14). Meanwhile, his masterly work on the social dynamics of suicide was an excellent example of how to relate deeply personal and private dilemmas to the development of the wider society (Durkheim 1951).

The British social researchers and reformers Sidney and Beatrice Webb also supported an emphasis on the use of documents in their guide to methods in social research, *Methods of Social Study*, published in 1932. The Webbs observed that social institutions possessed 'rich deposits of records about past and contemporary events which would be unobtainable by the methods of personal observation and statistical measurement' (1932, p. 98). In relation to their own research on the evolution of particular forms of social organisation, they insisted, 'an actual handling of the documents themselves must form the very foundation of any reconstruction or representation of events, whether of preceding periods or of the immediate past' (1932, p. 105). Indeed, they argued, 'it is only the documents, the writings secreted for the purpose of action, that yield authoritative evidence of the facts about the constitution and the activities of the social institutions to be studied' (1932, p. 106). The indefatigable Webbs confessed to finding a 'joy of life' in their 'diggings into documents and soundings and nettings of contemporaneous literature' (1932, p. 126), and concluded with a paean for document-based study as follows:

> To spend hour after hour in the chancel of an old parish church, in the veiled light of an ancient muniment room, in the hard little office of a solicitor, in the ugly and bare anteroom of the council chamber of a local authority, or even in a dungeon without ventilation or daylight (which was once our lot) with a stack of manuscripts, or a pile of printed volumes, to get through in a given time, induces an indescribably stimulated state of mind. The illusion arises that one has not one brain but several, each enjoying a life of its own.
>
> (Webb and Webb 1932, pp. 126–7)

This conviction may have been exceptional in its vigour, but it represented the commitment of a wide range of social researchers, especially in the inter-war years, to the study of social life through the documents generated by modern societies.

Estranging the familiar

Such studies, for all the differences between them and the faults they displayed, had in common an interdisciplinary approach to understanding modern communities, and an abiding interest in the influence of modern institutions and the State, and the social relationships of individuals. The critical use of a range of documents, both unsolicited and solicited by the researcher, was the bedrock of this kind of study. However, by the 1940s their fleeting pre-eminence was already beginning to be challenged by rival approaches to social research that relied on other types of evidence or data. This process reflected increasing specialisation in which some researchers began to focus with particular care on the position of individuals, while others chose to elaborate on the nature of the State. On the one hand, those who were preoccupied with individual, personal issues began to prefer a more direct approach than the use of documents allowed, that is, the face-to-face interview. This technique encouraged interaction with the individuals involved, and also the generation of new research data that were directly pertinent to the interests of the researcher rather than being patchy and haphazard in their relevance. On the other hand, those researchers who were more concerned with the overall development of states and societies rediscovered the use of statistical data, which had been dominant in the previous century.

The growing popularity of the interview method was already evident by the 1940s. In some social research of that period, interviewing and observation were employed as the key resources while documents provided additional material. This was the case, for example, in *The Social Life of a Modern Community*, produced by Warner and Lunt in 1941. Warner and Lunt emphasised the importance of adapting the techniques of ethnography and psychoanalysis as the basis for their study of 'Yankee City'. They argued that interviewing and observation, closely linked to each other, were the most useful methods for understanding the life of the community, just as they would be for anthropologists. However, they did acknowledge that these devices had some limitations. In particular, they were time-consuming and also it was impracticable to apply them to the society as a whole. Therefore, they noted that other sources, such as questionnaires and written documents, were also necessary, 'when the object of study has been carefully defined by observation and interview' (Warner and Lunt 1941, p. 55). The range of documents employed by Warner and Lunt was impressive, including as they did diaries, lists of subscribers and members of associations, directories, institutional records, annual reports and newspapers. They carefully explained the potential value of such source material:

> Partial diaries and scrapbooks containing details of the intimate life of the possessor were also collected. These yielded a mass of highly useful

and valuable material, covering the widest range of interests: poems which the individual had saved and memorised; speeches and sermons he thought expressed his belief in religion, politics, ethics, and other subjects of deep import to him; articles which gave his ideals of love and parenthood; and descriptions of national and local events which held his interest. The selection of materials in the scrapbooks of members of the ethnic groups clearly showed their ambivalent feelings about participation in the larger community. Interviews based on items from these sources greatly enhanced their value.

(Warner and Lynd 1941, p. 60)

Nevertheless, they had clearly been relegated to the second rank in terms of their importance to the study.

Even more strikingly, William Foote Whyte's *Street Corner Society*, first published in 1943, eschewed the use of documents in favour of participant observation. According to Whyte, it was not necessary to think in large-scale terms when addressing the concerns of individuals and groups, and he confined himself to observing their activities while becoming actively involved in them. As he himself reflected, 'I came to find that you could examine social structure directly through observing people in action' (Whyte 1943/1981, p. 285). Whyte's study was a model of the small-scale, qualitative approach to social research that favoured in-depth and direct examination of people in their social settings. Documents appeared to be of only marginal utility for such work because they allowed only indirect contact with people and groups, and a superficial understanding of their motivations and interactions. What Waller had described as the 'direct study of social phenomena' (1932/1967, preface) ultimately helped to lead social researchers away from documentary-based studies and towards an emphasis on interviews and observation.

Meanwhile, large-scale quantitative research based on surveys, question-naires and statistical data also began to regain popularity in the 1940s and 1950s. In the United States, Platt identifies a broad pattern of change over the period 1920–60 'towards increasing quantification in an increasing body of systematic empirical research in which sociologists have created their own data' (Platt 1996, p. 123). With regard to Britain, Finch (1986) has suggested that the dominant tradition of social and educational research from the 1830s onwards had been quantitative in nature. It was challenged by an alternative approach that emphasised qualitative methods, repre-sented for example by the organisation Mass Observation from 1937 until 1949, but after the Second World War large-scale statistically based social research was reaffirmed through the 'political arithmetic' espoused by researchers such as A.H. Halsey and Anthony Heath (see for example Halsey, Floud and Anderson, 1961; Halsey, Heath and Ridge, 1980). According to Finch, therefore,

The recurring themes are: the impartial collection of facts; an unproblematic conception of 'facts', based on a positivist epistemology; a
belief in the direct utility of such facts in shaping measures of social
reform which can be implemented by governments; and a strong preference for statistical methods and the social survey as the most suitable
technique for fact-collecting.

(1986, p. 37)

Thus, for example, Mass Observation itself became marginalised partly
because it was 'constantly vulnerable to criticisms informed by a view of
quantitative and survey work as the standard against which all research
should be measured' (Finch 1986, p. 99). This dominant tradition, as strong
as ever from the 1950s, tended to marginalise and downgrade not only qualitative approaches in general but also, and more particularly, document-
based studies of education and society.

By the 1960s, therefore, the use of documents in social research had
become unpopular and unfashionable. According to Eugene Webb and his
colleagues, interviews and questionnaires were generally regarded as preferable to documents in the 'dominant mass' of social science research, to the
extent that written documents were one of the 'underdeveloped data
resources of social science' (Webb *et al.* 1966, pp. 1, 104). There is a sense
in which documents fell from favour during this period as a principal technique of social research because they were too familiar. Abundant in their
profusion and ubiquitous in their propinquity, they could easily be taken
for granted as a means of finding out about the social world. Familiarity
could breed a form of contempt, as it seemed almost too simple and
straightforward to base a study on such readily available sources. As Silverman has suggested, for example,

Even in qualitative research, texts are sometimes only important as
'background material' for the 'real' analysis. Where texts are analysed,
they are often presented as 'official' or 'common-sense' versions of
social phenomena, to be undercut by the underlying social phenomena
apparently found in the qualitative researcher's analysis of her inter-
viewees' stories. The model is: the documents *claim* X, but we can
show that Y is the case.

(Silverman 2001, p. 119)

Equally, documents could appear to others overwhelming in their sheer
volume, comprising a deluge of data too extensive to offer ease of study or
analysis. Researchers turned instead to avenues that appeared more novel
and challenging, as well as more interesting in their capacity to engage
directly either with people or with the general issues of the day.

More profoundly, nevertheless, documents despite their basic familiarity became estranged from social researchers in a number of respects. First, they appeared better suited to the study of the past rather than of the present, because they had survived from previous periods of time whether recent or ancient. For this reason, they tended to become the preserve of historical researchers rather than of students of contemporary society. For historians, the document was the staple of research. Increasingly, documentary-based study became associated with historical approaches as opposed to social research. This in itself reflected a growing specialisation of academic labour based on the separate disciplines. It was also the harbinger of a demarcation, even an alienation, in the study of society between the past and the present. The Webbs had been dismissive of the idea of the present, describing it as 'a mere point between two eternities', the past and the future (Webb and Webb 1932, p. 105). Nevertheless, as social researchers became increasingly preoccupied with contemporary changes, the past often came to be regarded as arcane and even irrelevant to the problems at hand.

Secondly, the bureaucratic records of the modern state were designed to illuminate the official and public outlooks of the social and political elite. They were essentially top-down in nature. They were extensive, often pedantically and even obsessively so, on the administration of systems, whether at national, local or institutional level. They were less forthcoming on the effects of such deliberations on individuals and families, and were even less helpful for an understanding of social groups that were excluded or marginalised. They seemed to offer little for researchers who were more interested in the private lives of ordinary people.

A third issue concerns the nature of the research process involving documentary sources. Sidney and Beatrice Webb may have found a 'joy of life' in poring over documents, but others found it mysterious, frustrating and boring. Documents represented evidence that researchers did not produce for themselves, but which was already in existence. This meant that they were often not concerned directly with the issues that interested the researcher. It was possible to spend many hours, days or weeks studying them with little result. Also, whether they were located in a library, a records office or an attic, spending time with them meant being locked away from the world outside. Such a lonely, solitary and ultimately unsociable activity could easily seem a peculiar means of understanding more about society.

Document-based study thus gained an unenviable reputation for being esoteric, dry and narrow. At the same time, it became associated with the past rather than with the present, with the elite rather than with mass society, and with what C. Wright Mills (1959) would have described as 'public issues' as opposed to 'private troubles'. A historical tradition of document-based study asserted itself in the middle years of the twentieth century that was the negation of social inquiry into the concerns of ordinary people. The prime exponent of this historical approach was Sir Lewis

Namier, whose field of special expertise was politics in eighteenth-century England. In one of his major works, *The Structure of Politics at the Accession of George III*, first published in 1920, he emphasised his preoccupation with the politics of the elite class as opposed to the concerns of the populace. Towards this end, he made use of a large number of collections of private documents, listed in detail not at the end but at the front of the book. These included ten manuscript collections based in the British Museum in London, two in the Bodleian Library in Oxford, one in the County Record Office in Truro, another in the Huntington Library in California, another in Northamptonshire Record Office, another in the Public Record Office in London, yet another in the Royal Institution of Cornwall, and a further twenty-five in private family collections around Britain (Namier 1960, pp. vi–vii). The historian Linda Colley has observed that Namier was most interested in the sociology of elites, and the intrigues and conflicts among men in high office, but showed little interest in their use of power. His approach to documentary research focused on individual politicians, particularly through a detailed study of their correspondence. This was an approach that was unattractive to many historians who avoided the study of eighteenth-century England both in schools and in universities because of Namier's influence over the field (Colley 1989, p. 98). If Namierite history became the dominant image of documentary research, it would have alienated social researchers who had an interest in understanding the priorities and concerns of ordinary people and the structures of modern society.

Namier's approach was imitated by a number of disciples who were even narrower and more elitist in their concerns. For example, Maurice Cowling's book *The Impact of Labour 1920–1924*, published in 1971, was reliant on the letters and diaries of politicians, which the author regarded as crucial for an understanding of the political system in the period under discussion. These were drawn from over fifty collections held in different locations around Britain. From this source material, Cowling was able to reconstruct the character of high politics in these years. He was concerned exclusively with the relationships and manoeuvres of fifty or sixty politicians who had authority over the political process. As he warned at the start of his book, other politicians and the views of the political parties were not his concern, civil servants would hardly figure at all and issues of substance would be treated only in their relation to the standing of the governments and politicians concerned with them. For Cowling, the key to understanding the politics of the period was 'in the minds of the politicians who exercised ostensible power and in the relationship they envisaged with the society they wished to rule' (Cowling 1971, p. 11). Moreover, even when focusing on the network of powerful politicians at the heart of his study, Cowling evinced little interest in their personal lives and biographies, but only in their public and official positions within the short period of time under study.

By the late twentieth century, then, social research had become largely alienated from documentary studies. Unlike in the interwar period, when documentary study was a central and pervasive part of social research, it was now relatively marginal and unpopular. From the days of the Chicago school and the major arguments over the use of personal documents, a general decline had set in that appeared irretrievable. In its place, for social research, was an emphasis on surveys, direct observation and interviews. At the same time, historians were left to address the effects of a narrow and elitist approach to documentary studies that was widely unpopular. In the process, social research and history became alienated from each other. Past and present were disconnected, while the intimate relationships between the public and the private that had been closely observed in earlier work were rarely to be seen. The full potential of documentary research had lain precisely in the way that it could provide insights into these connections, between past and present on the one hand, and between public and private on the other. Its decline lay ultimately in the fragmentation of these basic core elements. Perhaps a rediscovery of the uses of documents in social research may depend on a renewed appreciation of the connections that they enable us to find.

Suggestions for further reading

Blumer, H. (1939) *An Appraisal of Thomas and Znaniecki's* The Polish Peasant in Europe and America, Critiques of Research in the Social Sciences, I: Social Science Research Council, New York

Finch, J. (1986) *Research and Policy: The Uses of Qualitative Methods in Social and Educational Research*, Falmer, London

Lynd, R. and Lynd, H. (1929) *Middletown: A Study in American Culture*, Constable, London

Platt, J. (1996) *A History of Sociological Research Methods in America, 1920–1960*, Cambridge University Press, Cambridge

Thomas, W.I. and Znaniecki, F. (1918–20/1927) *The Polish Peasant in Europe and America*, Dover Publications, New York

Webb, S. and Webb, B. (1932) *Methods of Social Study*, Longmans, Green and Co., London

3 The Joy of Life

Doing Documentary Research

The use of documents, increasingly neglected by social researchers as we saw in the last chapter, has become largely the preserve of historians. As Scott observed (1990, p. 1), 'The handling of documentary sources – government papers, diaries, newspapers and so on – is widely seen as the hallmark of the professional historian, whereas the sociologist has generally been identified with the use of questionnaires and interview techniques.' It is logical therefore to look to historians for advice on how to approach different kinds of documents, and especially on the key distinction between *primary* and *secondary* sources (see also McCulloch and Richardson 2000, chapters 5–6, on general issues relating to primary and secondary documents). Established precepts of working historians can be applied more broadly to educational and social research. On the other hand, contemporary changes are also very important to take into account as these are currently transforming the nature of document-based research. The growing popularity of edited versions of documents in published form has established a kind of *hybrid* source that is convenient for researchers but requires careful appraisal. Moreover, the Internet and electronic mail have created a new kind of document, the *virtual* source, which has major implications for the future of such research. Only by recognising the significance of these new developments can we begin to respond to the challenges and opportunities of doing documentary research in the twenty-first century.

What is a primary document?

A measure of the rapid changes that are transforming the nature of documentary research is that the distinction between the 'primary' and the 'secondary' source, for so long an unchallengeable construct, is coming to appear increasingly problematic. Certainly, historians continue to defend this as a fundamental distinction, sometimes obdurately, at other times more flexibly. Yet the basic dualism of primary and secondary sources seems in some respects to be an inadequate means of understanding the nature of documents, and their limitations and potential for understanding the social world.

A prime example of a historian who would maintain a sharp distinction between primary and secondary documentary sources is Arthur Marwick, who has published widely on British social history in the twentieth century (see for example Marwick 1965, 1968). In his influential work *The Nature of History* (Marwick 1970), Marwick explains the differences involved in vigorous and often combative style. Primary sources constitute 'the basic, raw, imperfect evidence', which is often fragmentary, scattered and difficult to use (Marwick 1970, p. 131). Secondary sources are the books and articles of other historians. As Marwick notes,

> At a common-sense level the distinction between a primary and a secondary source is obvious enough: the primary source is the raw material, more meaningful to the expert historian than to the layman; the secondary source is the coherent work of history, article, dissertation or book, in which both the intelligent layman and the historian who is venturing upon a new research topic, or keeping in touch with new discoveries in his chosen field, or seeking to widen his general historical knowledge, will look for what they want.
>
> (Marwick 1970, p. 132)

Marwick credits the nineteenth-century German school of historical writing, led by Berthold Georg Niebuhr and Leopold von Ranke, with establishing the 'scientific' study of primary sources. Ranke described the sources for his work as comprising 'memoirs, diaries, letters, diplomatic reports, and original narratives of eye-witnesses; other writings were used only if they were immediately derived from the above mentioned or seemed to equal them because of some original information' (Ranke 1970, p. 57). In other words, Ranke regarded primary documents, produced by eye-witnesses and participants in events, as superior to secondary sources.

In the most recent edition of his work, Marwick (2001) responds to growing scepticism about the distinction between primary and secondary sources in forceful fashion, to emphasise a rigid and fundamental divide between the two types:

> The distinction between primary and secondary sources is absolutely explicit, and is not in the least bit treacherous and misleading . . . The distinction is one of nature – primary sources were created within the period studied, secondary sources are produced *later*, by historians studying that earlier period and making use of the primary sources created within it.
>
> (Marwick 2001, p. 156)

Any misunderstanding on this score, according to Marwick, is due to ignorance or inexperience:

> The critics attack the distinction partly because they are secretly embarrassed that they themselves actually have no experience of what it is like to work among primary sources in the archives, and partly because many of them subscribe to the view that everything, primary or secondary, belongs to the single category 'text' and shares in the (invented and nonsensical) quality of 'textuality'.
>
> (Marwick 2001, p. 155)

Marwick also elaborates on this important notion of a hierarchy of documentary sources. Among secondary sources, as he suggests, academic monographs carry greater authority than sensationalised popular work. Moreover, according to Marwick, a hierarchy also operates within the broad category of primary sources. This, he contends, is based on the principle that 'something which is handwritten, and of which there may be only one copy, is somehow more *primary* than something which is printed, and of which there may be many copies' (Marwick 1970, pp. 132–3; emphasis in original). Moreover, he adds,

> Behind this idea there lies the more fundamental and perfectly reasonable one that the historian who has searched around, travelled far, written the necessary ingratiating letters to secure access to a rare document, has put in more man-hours than the historian who has relied on printed documents obtainable in all the major libraries (I am not here referring to a printed edition of the rare document, but to, for example, a government paper which began life in print and in many copies).
>
> (Marwick 1970, p. 133)

On this basis, manuscript materials held in archives and private collections would occupy the first level of the hierarchy of primary documentary sources, followed at the next level by published pamphlets, periodicals, government reports and reports of parliamentary debates which can be located in a university library or reading room. In this sense, unpublished and relatively inaccessible documents appear to carry greater intrinsic worth to the historical researcher than published documents that are widely available.

None the less, the notion of a clearly defined classification of types of documents is beset with a number of problems. First of these is the well recognised issue that many documents do not fit straightforwardly into such established patterns. Autobiographies, for example, are primary documents in the sense that the author is an eye-witness or participant in the events being discussed. On the other hand, they are produced in many cases years or decades after the event, and so may be inaccurate owing to failures of memory or selective recall. Such documents might well be regarded as less 'primary' than letters, diaries or memoranda produced immediately after the event, and indeed John Tosh affirms that the historian will usually prefer those sources that are closer in time and place to the events in question (Tosh 2002, p. 57).

At the same time, autobiographies may also be appraised as a secondary source in that they often seek to analyse the changing times through which the autobiographer has lived (Marwick 1970, p. 134). The autobiography of the leading educational historian Brian Simon, *A Life in Education* (2000), is an interesting example of this dual function. It includes reminiscences of his own experiences, for example as a teacher in different schools in Manchester in the late 1940s and as a lecturer and then professor at Leicester University. At the same time, it relates these experiences to broader educational, social and political movements over this time to develop a critique of continuing educational inequalities and to argue for change. This is informed in turn by historical perspectives and interpretations:

> Historical study over these years has shown that periods of education in the past have too often been followed by powerful and deliberate moves to turn back the clock – or to direct breakthroughs into innocuous channels . . . The need now is to go even further, and finally create a genuinely national system of education. Current provisions, historically based, are no longer acceptable. Such must be the agenda for the future.
>
> (Simon 2000, p. 176)

The supposed differences between primary and secondary sources are particularly obscure in such cases.

There are other ways also in which particular sources may be seen as both 'primary' and 'secondary' in nature. A scholarly work may be read as a contribution to its field or an approach to a specific problem, and thus as a secondary source, but also as a reflection of attitudes to issues in a particular context or period, or in other words as a primary document. Even Marwick in his most rigid mode concedes this point. As he notes, 'Self-evidently, a book which was a secondary source in the nineteenth century will normally not remain a useful secondary source for students in the twenty-first century, but may, if they are studying certain rather narrow aspects of the nineteenth century, become a primary source for them' (Marwick 2001, p. 156). For example, Fred Clarke's work *Education and Social Change*, published in 1940, is a significant study in terms of the sociology and history of education in England. At the same time, it is highly revealing in the way that it expresses an approach to the contemporary issues raised by the Second World War. He was concerned to encourage an adaptation of educational institutions following the war in a fashion that was consistent with his ideals of the English character or tradition (Clarke 1940). The book may be read and understood in either or both of these ways, depending on the interests of the reader.

There are also a large number of works that are edited versions of diaries, letters and autobiographies. Such sources perform an important role in helping to make documents that may be inaccessible or difficult to read much more widely available. On the other hand, the editing process may alter significant characteristics of the original primary document, whether in a subtle or in a systematic manner. As Robert Fothergill observed in his study of English diaries, editors who are engaged in producing a publishable work are prone to emphasise particular types of material, to make it more interesting to a general audience, or more flattering to the author, or to reflect particular interests (Fothergill 1974, p. 5). Such published versions of primary documents might therefore be regarded as hybrid in nature, the primary characteristics of the original document being compromised by the process involved in bringing it to public attention.

An example of this process is Ben Pimlott's two-volume published version of the diaries of a twentieth-century British Labour Party politician, Hugh Dalton. The original documents were deposited in the British Library of Political and Economic Science at the London School of Economics soon after Dalton's death in 1962. They consist of fifty-six notebooks and folders, amounting to more than one and a half million words. Pimlott's edited version divides the papers into the period of the coalition government in the Second World War (1940–45), which make up one volume, and Dalton's political career before and after the war (1918–40, 1945–60), which together make up the second (Pimlott 1986a, 1986b). The editor's explanation of his criteria for inclusion of material in the published version is engagingly frank. He acknowledges the difficulties involved, especially in view of the fact that a particular line in an 'otherwise colourless' paragraph might provide a 'vital link' (Pimlott 1986b, p. xxi). Where a passage of the diary had been previously included or closely paraphrased in Dalton's own autobiography, Pimlott generally omitted it from the published version. Thus for example there is very little on Dalton's period as Chancellor of the Exchequer from 1945 to 1947, important though it is, because this is already available in the autobiography (Pimlott 1986b, p. xxi). The effect is that the published diary aims to complement the three volumes of Dalton's memoirs and therefore needs to be read alongside them (Dalton 1953, 1957, 1962; Pimlott 1986a, 1986b).

In relation to the Second World War diary, moreover, Pimlott includes little on Dalton's role at the Ministry of Economic Warfare and the Board of Trade. Instead, he concentrates on the war, and on politics. He continues: 'I have included a lot of gossip about operations, and about colleagues; some of Dalton's careful records of talks with leading foreign exiles – especially Poles, with whom he was particularly close – and as much material as possible that relates to the wider background of the war. I have paid special attention to tensions and manoeuvrings within the Coalition, and to the activities of the Labour Party' (Pimlott 1986a, pp. xxxvii–xxxviii). The result is a coherent and readable work that systematically omits large and significant areas of Dalton's work, and which emphasises gossip and high politics at the expense of social and economic issues. Social researchers, while gaining much that is of benefit from the published version, might still need to make the journey to London to read the original.

There are many similar examples of this kind of editorial process. In the published version of the 'diary letters' of Austen Chamberlain, a British Conservative politician of the early twentieth century, the letters are abridged, according to the editor, 'to exclude much material of an interesting, but essentially non-political nature' (Self 1995, p. viii). In the diaries of Richard Crossman, a British Labour Party politician of the 1950s and 1960s, edited by Janet Morgan, the published work omits local material, accounts of journeys and visits, and discussions of particular areas of policy such as education and municipal ownership, as well as passages that 'seemed libellous or in bad taste' (Morgan 1981, p. 14). Even in the case of the eleven-volume published version of the diary of Samuel Pepys in the seventeenth century, which provides a full transcription of the original, the editors freely concede shortcomings in the process of translating the original into published form (Latham and Matthews 1970, p. xiv).

Online documents

Thus, edited versions of documents pose a significant challenge to received notions of primary and secondary sources. None the less, surely the greatest challenge to this basic distinction emanates from the new computer technology in the form of the World Wide Web, the Internet and electronic mail. Together, these provide unprecedented access to documents which hitherto had been available only to a few. They allow rapid (if not always instant) communication of large amounts of information on a global scale. They also promise to revolutionise the process involved in doing documentary research. Rather than being obliged often to travel long distances to gain access to archives and private collections, in many cases it will be possible for researchers to study the documents on their own computer screen. The emergence of virtual documents, stored electronically rather than on paper, heralds a new age for documentary-based studies. It brings with it exciting new opportunities for documentary research. It may also give rise to new problems, of which researchers need to be aware.

The leading historian Simon Schama has evoked the extraordinary potential of the World Wide Web to transform the nature of documentary research. He points out that the Internet can carry material which 'changes the conventional definition of documentation', but is still 'absolutely as substantial as the texts of treaties and parliamentary transcripts' (Schama 1999). Moreover, he predicts, 'the eventual, in some cases, imminent arrival of digital archives and the accessibility of these primary source materials not just to the academy, but to any informed lay user, may well be the biggest democratizer of historical knowledge since the invention of printed data' (Schama 1999). Nevertheless, Schama tempers his enthusiasm for the digital archive with a fondness for the established paper form: 'A click of the mouse won't give you the kick of seeing for the first time the faded ink on yellowing paper – of turning the distance of decades or centuries into finger-tip proximity' (Schama 1999). Such research potentially replaces the unsociable and secluded archive with the equally solitary pursuit of images on a computer screen in the privacy of the office.

There are many fascinating examples of new developments in the establishment of virtual archives. These very often undermine existing assumptions about documentary research. One such is the Centropa project, which seeks to combine oral history with family photographs. The aim is to put one thousand family histories relating to the Jewish communities of central Europe on to the Internet, alongside one hundred thousand pictures drawn from private collections. This will produce what is described as 'a timely cyber-museum giving a voice to the last generation of east European Jews who survived the Holocaust' (*The Guardian* 2003a). This project is particularly interesting for the way in which it sets out to convert life history interviews and family snapshots into documentary records. It establishes a close connection between the private suffering of so many Jewish families and the public tragedy of the Holocaust. It also relates the past to the present in a highly vivid fashion, evoking the changes and continuities of these communities over time and explaining their present hopes and fears. At the same time, it is inherently international, even global, in its nature, potentially available to any researcher with access to a computer connected to the Internet.

Another current example is the website http://www.movinghere.org.uk, launched in July 2003, which documents two hundred years of Caribbean, Irish, Jewish and South Asian migration to Britain. This site consists of over one hundred and fifty thousand digitised sources, including film, photographs and text, from thirty museums, libraries and archives. Selected ship passenger lists are included, searchable by name, and similar registers are provided of selected school and Home Office records. According to Sarah Tyacke, chief executive of the National Archives which took the lead in this project, there was a broader significance in such developments: 'Archives are moving away from their "dusty and musty" image by making these documents available at the click of a mouse' (*The Guardian* 2003b).

Another interesting case involves the British census of 1901, which the National Archive has placed in its entirety on to a website. This contains the details of more than 32 million British residents and their locations on 31 March 1901, the date of the census survey. These data were digitised from over 1.5 million pages listing the residents of Edwardian England and Wales, and include both the digitised images of the original hand-written pages, and the text, which has been transcribed electronically to make keyword searches possible (*The Observer* 2002; *The Guardian* 2002). Such was the level of public interest in this major initiative that the site had to be extensively upgraded over several months to respond to the demand. There was some scepticism expressed among professional search companies and genealogists, especially over the accuracy of such transcriptions, and a preference for the 'original document' over the virtual version. According to one family search company, for example, 'There are going to be problems with these transcriptions. Mistakes can completely ruin a search. People in this business have all had experience of this kind of hand-writing, and we know how difficult it can be. We will almost always want to see only the original documents' (*The Observer* 2002). Nevertheless, for many social researchers and millions of members of the public interested in tracing their own family histories, the online census was a major new resource with immense implications (the online census site can be located at http://www.pro.gov.uk/census).

One example of the kind of role that the online census can play concerns my own research on the life and career of the English educator Sir Cyril Norwood, which I have now been pursuing intermittently for the past fifteen years. At the time of the 1901 census Norwood was beginning his educational career, having just taken up a teaching post at Leeds Grammar School. It was therefore interesting but not particularly surprising to find that when the census was conducted Norwood was a lodger at 2 Woodsley Terrace in Leeds. I was much more taken aback when I looked for the details of Norwood's father, Samuel. According to the census material, Samuel was living with his wife, Elizabeth, in Leyton in Essex, where they had been settled for many years. Also resident in their house was a daughter, Mary, who was thirty-three years old and must have been the child of Samuel and his first wife, Sarah, who had died in October 1868. After many years of trawling diligently in the 'original documents', this was the first time that I had come across the fact that Cyril Norwood had an older half-sister from his father's first marriage; a fascinating piece of information about his family background which was a significant influence on his later career. Moreover, I had discovered this on a quiet weekend at my home computer with only minimal expense, rather than by travelling large distances for uncertain results.

The United Kingdom National Archive has also instituted an online service for a number of other records, including government papers. For example, it is possible to gain free access to confidential Cabinet meetings held by the British Conservative government in 1972. Included among these is an interesting discussion of education policy at the Cabinet meeting held on 30 November 1972 (see http://www.pro-online.pro.gov.uk, catalogue reference CAB 128/50/55). This discussion followed items on overseas issues such as the Icelandic fisheries dispute, which was then at its height, and industrial issues including the effects of Value Added Tax. For the item on education policy, the Cabinet at this meeting considered proposals put forward by the Secretary of State for Education and Science (Margaret Thatcher) and the Secretary of State for Scotland (Gordon Campbell). Thatcher explained the basis for a ten-year strategy for education that would be represented in a forthcoming White Paper, to be entitled *Education: A Framework for Expansion*. She pointed out that this would entail a major expansion of nursery education, a programme for improving or replacing obsolete secondary schools, an increase in the building programme for special schools for 'handicapped' children, improved arrangements for the training of probationary teachers and the in-service training of qualified teachers and, finally, the 'continued expansion of higher education, although at a rather lower rate'. Thatcher recommended this approach as 'a balanced programme for continued expansion'. Its provisions were within the agreed estimates for public expenditure, while for later years 'the programme was described in sufficiently flexible terms to avoid entailing a precise financial commitment'. The strategy proposed for the corresponding White Paper for education in Scotland was broadly similar.

The resultant discussion at this Cabinet meeting, as recorded in this note of its conclusions, generally welcomed these proposals:

> It was suggested that there might be some criticism of the proposed reduction in the rate of expansion of higher education; but the Cabinet were assured that the universities themselves were not likely to find the proposals unpalatable so far as student numbers were concerned, although they might be less satisfied as regards the implied restraints on unit costs. It must be accepted that the employment expectations of individuals entering higher education would have to be revised, since there were unlikely to be sufficient jobs in future at the level at present regarded as appropriate for graduates. Even so, the Government would need, in presenting the proposals to the public, to emphasise that, despite the adjustment of the education programme now envisaged, the expansion of higher education would continue; and, more generally, the positive aspects of the Government's policy should be stressed throughout the White Paper. In particular it should be made clear that the proposed major expansion in nursery education was not being achieved by abandoning expansion in any other direction. Appropriate arrangements, including Ministerial speeches and broadcasts in the

regions, should be made in order to secure the maximum presentational impact for a major development of the Government's social policies.

It was also noted that both White Papers should make clear that 'they were concerned primarily with the allocation of resources and with questions of organisation, not with the content of education'. This was because 'Otherwise it might be suggested that the Government were evading issues – for example, unruly behaviour in schools and the persistence of semi-illiteracy – about which there was considerable public concern.' A further point related to 'differences in emphasis' between the two White Papers on certain issues that it was feared 'might result in misunderstanding and, possibly, political embarrassment'. On this point, 'The Cabinet were assured, however, that these differences were defensible by reference to the respective educational systems of the two countries and should not give rise to significant criticism.' Moreover, in relation to the universities, 'It was agreed that, pending a definite decision on the possibility of relating tuition fees to economic costs and introducing a loan element into the support system for postgraduate students, it would be preferable to omit all reference to these topics'. The prime minister, Edward Heath, finally summed up the discussion on the two White Papers as follows:

> They represented a major policy initiative by the Government and should be presented as such. Their positive aspects should be stressed; and it should be made clear, in particular, that the proposed major expansion in nursery education would be accompanied by a continuance of the expansion of higher education and of the programmes for upgrading or replacing obsolete schools and for improving the numbers and training of teachers.
>
> (http://www.pro-online.pro.gov.uk, CAB 128/50/55)

Hence, online documents can often furnish valuable evidence for educational and social researchers. Indeed, they constitute a source that is potentially of immense significance for documentary research.

Many similar examples could be cited. However, in some cases researchers should treat this kind of documentary source with particular care. This occurs where government departments and other organisations have established their own website which is open to public access. These can again provide a wide range of useful information for researchers. For instance, the website of the Department for Education and Skills, in Britain (http://www.dfes.gov.uk), provides full details of events, departmental publications, statistics, legislation, policy issues and ministerial speeches. It includes an extensive archive section with speeches and policy papers for the past few years. The resource as a whole is fully searchable, although so large and complex that it can be confusing. This is a major resource, but it also has significant limitations for educational and social researchers. In particular, the information that it provides tends to cast the department and its ministers in a favourable light; indeed, this might be regarded as one of the main purposes of the website. It gives the official government perspective on the issues of the day, and the orthodox line to undermine criticisms and alternatives. Such is also the case with businesses and corporations (see also May 2001, p. 197). In the case of the DfES, an intriguing example is a short paper that was posted on the DfES website at the end of 2002 by the new Secretary of State for Education and Skills, Charles Clarke. This is included here in full (Case Study 2).

Case Study 2

Charles Clarke, Secretary of State for Education and Skills, UK Memorandum, Department for Education and Skills website, http://www.dfes.gov.uk/elite, n.d. [December 2002]

Elitism

I want to examine the word 'elitism' and to consider what it really means.

Elites are a fact of life.

All of our international sporting teams are elites. From Linford Christie to Paula Radcliffe, the English football team to Steve Redgrave our great sports people are by definition parts of an elite.

In the artistic world, the nation's great performers in the theatre, as popular singers or as film stars are all parts of an elite.

Our greatest national scientists – whether understanding the human genome, exploring the depths of space or identifying the impact of the process of climate change – are all parts of an intellectual elite.

Politicians are part of an elite. Members of Parliament are uniquely entitled to make the laws of this country and, in various ways, to try and hold the government of the day to account.

Judges, newspaper editors, chief executives of FTSE 100 companies, chief constables, hospital consultants, bishops and many others are all parts of different elites who influence the lives of the nation in a variety of ways.

These elites all have their important roles that they perform more or less well. I'd prefer to be operated on by an elite hospital consultant than by a second-rater, to be represented in international sports by world-class performers rather than an also-ran, to be taught in schools by outstanding teachers rather than by timeservers.

continued on next page

So I maintain that the problem is not that these elites exist. That's obvious and we should celebrate people who do well.

But we must ask important questions about elites. How does anyone join? What is the membership criteria? And how is the power of the elite used?

Any frank assessment of this country should acknowledge that for all of the elites I've mentioned, sports and arts, business and politics, research and teaching, our society does not reach out widely enough. There are literally millions of people who could contribute as part of elites but never have the opportunity to do so. The criteria therefore has to be merit not circumstance or inheritance.

Government's mission is not to get rid of the elites, whose talents we need in so many areas to improve our lives. Our mission is to do what we can to ensure that people from all walks of life get the chances to join these elites and that elites use their knowledge to benefit others.

We need more opportunities for the potentially world-class sports people who want to compete for Britain, more ability for clever children of all backgrounds to get a university education and become world-class researchers, more business entrepreneurs from every type of home background in the country.

And for the power elites in politics and elsewhere we need to open up our own structure to a far wider range of people. That's why in Government we're positively trying to change ourselves so that there will be more women in parliament and local councils, more from minority ethnic communities, more from genuine working backgrounds.

And as Secretary of State of Education and Skills I see one of my greatest responsibilities to be to offer every citizen the chance to be part of an elite judged on merit. To do this we must provide educational opportunities to fulfil their aspirations which, as appropriate may give them the chance of the elite which is right for them.

That's why we have our early years programme to attack disadvantage from birth; why we have focused on literacy and numeracy in primary schools, and will continue to do so. It's also why we are trying to build a secondary education system where the best schools and teachers collaborate with others so that every child has the chance to realise their potential, and a post-16 education system which allows everyone, throughout their lives, to get the opportunities to fulfil their hopes.

And at universities too, we need to recognise that there are many different elites from the soon-to-be-world class researchers to the first class medical students, from the brilliant and creative entrepreneurs to the top quality professionals.

continued on facing page

Our job is not to destroy these elites, but it is to do our best to ensure that the potential access to these elite groups is genuinely widely spread so that any child, from whatever community they come, can aspire to be part of the national and international elite in which they are interested.

All who want to argue about elitism should not focus upon the very existence of elites but upon the ways in which any elite is formed.

The Government has a very good record in this area. Government's policy really is to open up the elites wherever they exist and to give everyone a fair crack.

Let's not attack the bogey of elitism; let's do what we can to break down the divisive artificial barriers which still do exist in so many parts of our society.

Charles Clarke

This kind of document is attempting to persuade the reader to accept a particular policy or set of policies and, even more significantly, the philosophies that underpin them. In this it is like other documents, despite its virtual form and its status on a government department website. That is, whether one is reading primary or secondary documents, whether the documents are on paper or on the Internet, they need to be read critically and analysed rather than being taken at face value. This point leads in turn to a key issue in all documentary-based educational and social research: how to analyse a document.

Analysing documents

The historian John Tosh usefully encapsulates the difficulties involved in the analysis of documents, with particular reference to primary source material. According to Tosh, mastery of the sources is generally unattainable, not simply because they are so numerous, but because each of them requires so much careful appraisal. This is because, as he asserts,

> the primary sources are not an open book, offering instant answers. They may not be what they seem to be; they may signify very much more than is immediately apparent; they may be couched in obscure and antiquated forms which are meaningless to the untutored eye . . . Even for the experienced historian with green fingers, research in the primary sources is time-consuming; for the novice it can be painfully slow.
>
> (Tosh 2002, p. 86)

Nevertheless, there are some basic well established rules that apply in appraising and analysing documents, and these are generally discussed in terms of authenticity, reliability, meaning and theorisation.

The first, preliminary stage in this process is to establish the authenticity of the document. This means, as Scott observes, determining whether the evidence is 'genuine and of unquestionable origin' (Scott 1990, p. 6). Scott argues that this is a fundamental criterion in all social research, not simply for documentary research: 'Unless the researcher is able to come to a conclusion about the authenticity of the evidence, there is no possibility of an informed judgment about the quality of the data eventually constructed' (Scott 1990, p. 7). In the case of documents, the author, the place and the date of writing all need to be established and verified. This is partly to guard against the possibility that the document has been forged, but more usually to check whether the version that one is inspecting is correct and complete. Often the provenance or origins of the document may well be unproblematic, especially if the original version was produced in published form such as a public report, or if it is part of a collection held and catalogued in a reputable archive. On the other hand, in many cases errors in the document may arise, perhaps from being copied or reproduced from an original, and it is important to be alert to inconsistencies either within the document itself or in relation to the context in which it was produced (see for example Platt 1981).

When the authenticity of the document (or documents) has been established to the researcher's satisfaction, the next key stage is to appraise reliability, that is, how far its account can be relied on. This includes issues relating to truth and bias, but also the availability of relevant source material and the representativeness of those documents that have survived to be researched. An initial set of questions might be, Tosh suggests, to decide whether the author of the document was in a position to give a faithful account by being actually present at the event being depicted, set out while in a stable and attentive frame of mind, and recorded immediately after the event (Tosh 2002, pp. 91–2). The author of the document may also be too inexperienced or too inexpert for his or her account to be wholly trusted. So far as truth is concerned, the document may give a knowingly false outline of events that have been witnessed or an untrue assessment of a situation. It may be censored or bowdlerised, or omit important points perhaps to avoid incurring the displeasure of the reader/s for whom it was intended. Whether or not this is the case, there may well be an element of bias on the part of the author that the researcher needs to take into account. Bias may be produced by a wide range of possible motives: to rationalise one's own actions, and to discredit those of others; to support a case or to undermine it; to understate a problem or to exaggerate it. Biased accounts are certainly not to be ignored, not simply because this would leave few if any sources of documentary evidence for the researcher, but also because an understanding of the biases involved gives the researcher a significant clue to the issues being studied.

Another aspect of the reliability for the documentary researcher concerns the differential survival rate of documents. Webb *et al.* (1966) note that two major sources of bias are what they call 'selective deposit' and 'selective survival'. Some documents are more likely than others to be stored safely after they have been produced. For example, the bureaucratic records of the State in western nations are housed in public archives, well guarded and meticulously catalogued. Many other documents are routinely discarded. Over the years, moreover, some documents are more likely than others to survive unharmed, although accidents such as fire and flood can damage even the best-guarded national repository. Increasing use of electronic communications such as electronic mail may well compound the problem of document survival, although in practice many users of email routinely retain at least the key documents produced by this means, and often successive drafts of correspondence or reports.

In consequence, the researcher is likely to have only a small proportion of relevant documentary sources actually available for study. Thus, Platt complains: 'Some documents one might like to have will never have existed, others have been lost or destroyed, and others still exist but one cannot get access to them' (Platt 1981, p. 32). Andrew (1985) also laments:

> The answers to a great many questions are simply not available, since the necessary records either never existed or failed to survive. There is the frustration of events reported without follow up, individuals not clearly identified, ambiguous accounts or those which provide a wealth of detail except that which is desperately sought. Characters in the plot are 'lost'; do they die, move away, cease to be seen as of interest, or, in the case of women, marry and change their names? Diaries tell enough about people or events to underline their importance but no trace of them can be found elsewhere. Even more prosaically, the material which is so central to the research suddenly changes in character or runs out; the newspaper for a particular (crucial) week has been destroyed; the discovery in the record office catalogue of some immensely exciting document leads only to the information that it disappeared mysteriously five years ago, or is damaged beyond restoration. Material which might enable a wealth of insight can be tantalisingly elusive.
>
> (p. 156)

Documents that do survive in some quantity are probably strongest in presenting official viewpoints and those that have ultimately been successful, rather than those of subordinate and oppressed groups. Such factors lead to questions about how 'representative' or 'typical' or 'generalisable' are the documents that have survived to be studied. Webb *et al.* raise the issue of sampling error; for example, they contend,

> With the study of suicide notes, the question must be asked whether suicides who do not write notes would have expressed the same type of thoughts had they taken pen in hand. Any inferences from suicide notes must be hedged by the realisation that less than a quarter of all suicides write notes. Are both the writers and nonwriters drawn from the same population?
>
> (Webb *et al.* 1966, p. 55)

Scott (1990) is also much exercised by this kind of problem. He recognises that typicality is not always required, but insists that the researcher needs to know how typical the available evidence is in order to be able to assign limits to the application of any conclusions that are drawn from it (Scott 1990, p. 7).

Several writers have suggested that, in order to overcome these potential problems of reliability and bias, it is necessary to make use of a wide range of different kinds of documents which will represent alternative viewpoints and interests. At times this process appears to be conceived as a form of triangulation, through which the truth will emerge from testing different kinds of documents against each other. According to Tosh, for instance, historical researchers should not be dependent on a single source, for it is likely to be in some way inaccurate, incomplete or otherwise tainted. Instead, he continues,

> The procedure is rather to amass as many pieces of evidence as possible from a wide range of sources – preferably from *all* the sources that have a bearing on the problem in hand. In this way the inaccuracies and distortions of particular sources are more likely to be revealed, and the inferences drawn by the historian can be corroborated. Each type of source possesses certain strengths and weaknesses; considered together, and compared one against the other, there is at least a chance that they will reveal the true facts – or something very close to them.
>
> (Tosh 2002, p. 98)

The assumptions inherent in this argument are rather intriguing, and exemplify the general 'absence of epistemological discussion from the writings of historians on these matters' (Platt 1981, p. 40). Indeed, as Platt remarks, 'It is not feasible, except possibly in very unusual circumstances, simply to subtract the erroneous parts and to proceed securely on the basis of the remainder, both because of the likelihood that there would be no remainder, and because even if probable error can be identified it is not always thereby evident what would be correct' (Platt 1981, p. 40). In addition, a single document, or a set of documents from the same source or author, might well be valuable to the researcher in that it helps to reconstruct the experiences and changing ideas and practices of one particular individual, or family, or party or other entity, however typical or atypical it may be.

A further general issue concerns the meaning of the document. This involves ensuring that the evidence is clear and comprehensible to the researcher (Scott 1990, p. 8). However, there are a number of further points that are relevant in this connection. It has often been stressed, for instance, that researchers should give attention to the context in which the document was produced. Marwick notes that historians should satisfy themselves that they have understood the document as its contemporaries would have understood it, rather than as it would be understood today (Marwick 1981, pp. 145–6). This entails recognition of technical phrases, esoteric allusions and references to individuals and institutions, as well as of the changing usages of particular words and terms.

In recent years, there has been increasing emphasis on the nature of the document itself as a text, especially of its language and form, in determining its deeper meaning, following the principles of hermeneutics (Punch 1998, p. 231; May 2001, pp. 183–5). For example, Fairclough has developed a social semiotic approach to documents that seeks to understand the language and other kinds of symbols and images in the text. This includes studying the form and organisation of the document as well as its content, and its absences or silences no less than what is included. He also attempts to relate the document to an understanding of social practice, arguing that the 'discourse' of a document represents 'language seen as a form of social practice' (Fairclough 1995, p. 20). Moreover, as well as linguistic analysis Fairclough also identifies intertextual analysis as a key focus for social researchers, entailing a comparative understanding of the discourses of different texts in relation to social change. Some historians have also promoted the 'linguistic turn', as this recourse to detailed study of the language and discourse of the document is often called. Sol Cohen, for example, suggests that documents should be understood in terms of 'the semiotics of text production, how meaning is made in text, how readers take meaning from text, the status of authorial intention versus the reader's interpretation, the role of the community of discourse in the reception of text, and so forth' (Cohen 1999, pp. 65–6). Cohen himself goes so far as to argue that there is no single correct approach to reading a historical text, only different ways of reading it (Cohen 1999, p. 81). This relates closely also to some recent discussions of how practitioners read the texts of policy. For example, Bowe and Ball (1992), drawing on the work of Roland Barthes, insist that 'Practitioners do not confront policy texts as passive readers, they come with histories, with experience, with values and purposes of their own, they have vested interests in the meaning of policy . . . The simple point is that policy writers cannot control the meanings of their texts' (p. 22).

These considerations of meaning begin to intrude on the final aspect of document analysis, which is theorisation. This entails developing a theoretical framework through which to interpret the document. Jupp and Norris (1993) propose three broad traditions in documentary analysis within which particular types of theoretical approach may be located: positivist, interpretive and critical. The positivist approach emphasises the objective, rational, systematic and quantitative nature of the study. The interpretive outlook stresses the nature of social phenomena such as documents as being socially constructed. The critical tradition is heavily theoretical and overtly political in nature, emphasising social conflict, power, control and ideology, and includes Marxist and feminist theory and, latterly, critical modes of discourse analysis.

An example of a positivist approach to the use of documents might be Halstead's examination of a controversy in England in the mid-1980s in which the headteacher Ray Honeyford became a focus of contention over multicultural education (Halstead 1988). In the interests of 'objectivity' and 'thoroughness', Halstead examined, compared and cross-referenced virtually every local and national newspaper, magazine and journal article produced on the 'Honeyford affair', amounting to well over one thousand articles, and supported this with reference to original documents produced by the local education authority and relevant pressure groups (Halstead 1988, p. 83). These contributions are set out and explained in a fifty-three-page appendix to the work. However, the author makes little attempt to provide a deeper analysis in terms of differential power, influence or ideologies of the various groups that these documents represent, and the impression is left that the sum of all the relevant papers will add up to an objective account.

An example of an approach to documentary research with interpretive and critical elements is the work of John Codd (1988) on the construction and deconstruction of educational policy documents. Codd identifies what he calls a 'technical-empiricist' view of policy making in which policy statements and documents relate the values and goals of education policy to factual information arising from research. The analysis of the documents based on this perspective sets out to establish the correct interpretation of the text. Codd argues that such an approach is founded on mistaken idealist assumptions about the intentions of policy and the character of language, which are themselves founded upon a liberal humanist ideology that tends to obscure the contradictions underlying state policies (Codd 1988, p. 237). As an alternative approach, he emphasises theories of discourse that relate the use of language to the exercise of power, and seeks to deconstruct the official discourse as 'cultural and ideological artefacts to be interpreted in terms of their implicit patterns of signification, underlying symbolic structures and contextual determinants of meaning' (p. 243). Thus, for example, the *Curriculum Review* produced by the New Zealand Education Department in March 1987 as a 128-page policy document is deconstructed by focusing on 'the processes of its production as well as on the organisation of the discourses which constitute it and the strategies by which it masks the contradictions and incoherences of the ideology that is inscribed in it' (p. 245). Such an analysis, according to Codd, helps to ascertain the actual and potential effect of the text upon its readers, rather than to establish the intended meaning of its authors. This will tend to suggest a plurality of meanings ascribed to the text among different categories of readers, but, as Codd concludes,

> The aim of discourse analysis is not to prove which of these readings is *correct* but to consider them *all* as evidence of the text's inherent ideological ambiguities, distortions and absences. In this way, it is possible to penetrate the ideology of official policy documents and expose the real conflicts of interest within the social world which they claim to represent.
>
> (Codd 1988, p. 246)

Codd's account therefore understands the policy document as being socially constructed as in the interpretive standpoint, but goes beyond this to make use of critical discourse theory in challenging the ideology and underlying contradictions of the policy itself.

Purvis's approach to historical documentary research from a feminist perspective (1985) is also a useful instance of a critical interpretation. Purvis conceives her research in terms of a challenge to male definitions of knowledge. It involved trying to find documentary sources of different types, including official texts, published commentary and reporting, and personal texts, many of which had not survived because they were often deemed to be not worth preserving. According to Purvis, 'The feminist undertaking documentary research into the past has to go back to the primary sources and be a "better" detective than many other researchers have been before because an analysis of the situation of women and of the power relationships between the sexes has been "hidden" and "obscured"' (Purvis 1985, p. 200). The task of the feminist documentary researcher is therefore to expose and question 'the sexist assumptions within malestream academic disciplines', as well as to promote an awareness of the experience of women in the past and in the present (Purvis 1985, pp. 200–1).

These different aspects of analysing documents should not be conceived as wholly separate or distinct, despite the presentation here and in the existing literature, still less as chronologically consecutive. In practice they overlap and interact with each other. Moreover, it is important for us to understand documentary-based research as being, like other forms of educational and social research, not a linear model but a social process (see for example Burgess 1984b). Further reflexive accounts are needed of the social process and personal experience of documentary research. Some of the best and most useful of these, by Ivor Goodson (1985), Alison Andrew (1985), June Purvis (1985) and Rene Saran (1985), were published together in a collection edited by Robert Burgess (1985), and a recent example would be Steedman (2001). Nonetheless, there have been relatively few of these to set alongside the many first-person accounts of ethnographic research projects (e.g. Walford 2001).

Legal frameworks and ethical issues

In the conduct of documentary research it is most important to be aware of and to abide by the rights, responsibilities and restrictions conferred in the prevailing legal provisions. These vary greatly from one nation to another, and are often subject to considerable change. At the same time, a potentially key issue in document analysis that has been neglected as a result of the general lack of recognition of documentary research as a social process is the ethical dimension of such research. This may appear to be less important than in other types of educational and social research, partly because it does not involve a direct interaction with respondents, and partly because it often concerns events and people from the past rather than those of today. None the less, in many cases there are serious ethical issues to be considered in documentary research.

Among the most significant dimensions of the legal framework that affect documentary researchers are copyright, freedom of information and data protection. In the British context, all of these have received considerable attention over the past decade, with important implications for researchers. The Copyright, Designs and Patents Act of 1988 covers literary, dramatic, musical and artistic works for seventy years from the death of the last remaining author or from the first publication of the work, after which time it falls into the public domain. This applies to computer files and data on the Internet as well as to paper documents (for a copy of the 1988 Act with amendments see http://www.swarb.co.uk/acts/1988CopyDesPatAct. html). In terms of personal information, the Data Protection Act of 1998 embodies far-reaching provisions designed especially to protect details of personal data or identification of particular individuals from being published during the lifetime of the individual (see for details of the 1998 Act http://www.hmso.gov.uk/acts/acts1998/19980029.htm). At the same time, the Freedom of Information Act (2000) is a further key piece of legislation that allows researchers to gain access to government and institutional records on application depending on a number of caveats (see http:// www.hmso.gov.uk/acts/acts2000/20000036.htm). Considerations of confidentiality of information and the intellectual ownership of data are sensitive issues that must be clarified at an early stage of the research (see also for example Townend 2000).

These legal requirements also relate closely to the ethical problems that can arise in documentary research. One instance of this is the issue of whether specific institutions and individuals should be identified in such research, especially for recent or current topics or in relation to private information or 'troubles' (Mills 1959). This might be problematic even for earlier periods. In my own research, I came across evidence from the family papers of Cyril Norwood that he had major problems during his time as Head of the leading English public (independent) school Harrow from 1926 until 1934, especially in the face of open opposition from several of his staff. In the case of one of these, the traditionalist C.G. Pope, he found the opposition so troubling that he forced Pope's early retirement from the staff. There may be a case for suggesting that a public disclosure of this kind of confidential and private material breaches ethical guidelines and might be hurtful and embarrassing, for the school or for surviving relatives and friends of the people involved. On the other hand, in this instance the school involved is a major, influential and prominent institution, the Head was also a leading figure in educational policy whose ideas were probably influenced by his difficulties at Harrow, and the official history of the school has already published details of this personal conflict (Tyerman 2000, pp. 509–11). The public issues involved might justify publication in such a case, but would the same be true for a less well known school or other institution, where the principal figures are not so clearly linked to broader concerns?

Ethical dilemmas might also arise in insider research based on documentary sources, access to which has been made possible through the researcher's position within the institution. The research may have been commissioned by the institution itself, in which case the researcher may be constrained from using material that might undermine or damage it, or from interpreting the documents in an unfavourable way. If the research is for an independent study, the researcher may still feel unable to cast aspersions on present or past colleagues, or may be vulnerable to being disciplined or dismissed if he or she does so. In such a circumstance, if such documents are used to question the practices or role of the institution, the researcher may be in a very difficult position. Researchers who are members of a government department, or of a major corporation, or even of a university, if they are researching their own institution, may thereby run the risk of being stigmatised as whistle-blowers. At the same time, such research may also be ethically problematic if it fails to report illegal or harmful activities (see also for example Potts 2000).

The reflections on doing documentary research in this chapter have built on established historical precepts about primary and secondary sources and a hierarchy of evidence. We have observed that many of the received assumptions about researching with documents have been challenged in recent times, partly because of the rise of hybrid sources, but especially with the emergence of the virtual document. The analysis of documents entails a number of considerations, many of which have been well rehearsed, but issues of theorisation and potential ethical dilemmas in particular raise problems that have often been left implicit or else ignored entirely.

This general account has also raised significant issues concerning the relationship between the past and the present, and between the public and the private domain. Much documentary-based research has explored historical problems, whether in the remote or the recent past, but the precepts developed in such research can also be applied to contemporary education and society. At the same time, theoretical concerns that are usually associated with the social sciences can be applied in order to problematise and develop the use of documents in ways to which historians are generally unaccustomed. So far as the public and private dimensions of society are concerned, we have seen a number of examples already of how documentary sources can often illuminate both 'private troubles' and 'public issues'. From the memoirs of Brian Simon to the evidence amassed on the Internet to the travails of Cyril Norwood at Harrow School, it is evident that documentary research can provide important insights into the tensions between the public and the private in contemporary societies. In the next chapter, we turn our attention to explore in more detail the extent to which records are able to advance our knowledge and understanding of such aspects.

Suggestions for further reading

Burgess, R. (ed.) (1985) *Strategies of Educational Research: Qualitative Methods*, Falmer, London

Codd, J. (1988) The construction and deconstruction of educational policy documents, *Journal of Education Policy*, 3/3, pp. 235–47

Jupp, V. and Norris, C. (1993) Traditions in documentary analysis. In M. Hammersley (ed.), *Social Research: Philosophy, Politics and Practice*, Sage, London, pp. 35–51

Marwick, A. (2001) *The New Nature of History: Knowledge, Evidence, Language*, Palgrave, London

Platt, J. (1981) Evidence and proof in documentary research, *Sociological Review*, 29/1, pp. 31–66

Tosh, J. (2002) *The Pursuit of History: Aims, Methods and New Directions in the Study of Modern History*, revised 3rd edn, Longman, London

http://www.pro.gov.uk/census

http://www.pro-online.gov.uk

http://www.dfes.gov.uk

4   Behind the Scenes

Records and Archives

Archives are the running record of society (Webb *et al.* 1966, p. 55) and the institutional memory of government (Archive New Zealand 2003). According to Pierre Nora (1996, p. 8), archives are the guardians of the memories of modern societies, which are increasingly dependent upon them:

> No previous epoch ever stocked archives at such a prodigious rate: modern society spews out greater volumes of paper than ever before, and we now possess unprecedented means for reproducing and preserving documents, but more than that, we feel a superstitious respect and veneration for the trace. As traditional memory has vanished, we have felt called upon to accumulate fragments, reports, documents, images, and speeches – any tangible sign of what was – as if this expanding dossier might some day be subpoenaed as evidence before who knows what tribunal of history. The trace negates the sacred but retains its aura.

Velody (1998) goes so far as to claim: 'As the backdrop to all scholarly research stands the archive. Appeals to ultimate truth, adequacy and plausibility in the work of the humanities and social sciences rest on archival presuppositions' (p. 1).

Yet it is also here that the intimidating nature of documentary research is at its most revealing. Jacques Derrida has referred allusively to 'Archive Fever', and to a frustrating and fruitless passion for what the archives may reveal of our societies and ourselves:

> It is to burn with a passion. It is never to rest, interminably, from searching for the archive right where it slips away. It is to run after the archive, even if there's too much of it, right where something inside of it anarchives itself. It is to have a compulsive, repetitive, and nostalgic desire for the archive, an irrepressible desire to return to the origin, a

homesickness, a nostalgia for the return to the most archaic place of absolute commencement.

(Derrida 1995, p. 57)

When Carolyn Steedman ponders on the physical and emotional effects of archive-based research, she evokes the day-to-day struggles that are familiar to many historians. She reflects thus on her efforts to find the 'myriads of the dead' encountered at the archive: 'You think: I could get to hate these people; and then: I can never do these people justice; and finally: I shall never *get it done*' (Steedman 2001, pp. 17–18). Steedman continues: 'Your craft is to conjure a social system from a nutmeg grater, and your competence in that was established long ago. Your anxiety is more precise, and more prosaic. It's about PT S2/1/1, which only arrived from the stacks that afternoon, which is enormous, and which you will never get through tomorrow' (Steedman 2001, p. 18). The massive amounts of documentary material stored in archives around the world have immense potential for educational and social researchers, but there is an underlying inhibition, even fear, that must be confronted in tapping these resources.

What is an archive?

Scott (1990) makes clear the basic requirements of an archive:

'Archival' access exists where the documents have been lodged in a place of storage which is open to all comers; researchers and the general public therefore may use an archive subject only to minimal administrative restrictions – such as the need to apply for a reader's ticket, supply references, and attend during opening hours – and can consult all documents lodged in that archive.

(p. 14)

Even these restrictions are challenged by web-based archives that have no need for readers' tickets, references and opening hours, but the essential purpose of storing documents for readers to consult still holds good in such cases. The *Oxford English Dictionary* defines the archive as 'A place in which public records or other important historic documents are kept' (1989, vol. I, p. 614). According to the *Encyclopaedia Britannica*, meanwhile, an archive or record office constitutes a 'repository for an organized body of records produced or received by a public, semipublic, institutional, or business entity in the transaction of its affairs and preserved by it or its successors' (Micropaedia, vol. 1, p. 530). None the less, archives are not only governmental or organisational in character, but can also be based on personal and private records. As Tyacke (2001, pp. 7–8) points out, 'They are all pervasive, as everyone either keeps records or is in one: you may be in a census and you will surely keep some form of written identification with you. Records (archives) can be prosaic, recording individual daily matters, or portentous, recording earth-shattering events.' It is possible to make a broad distinction between official documents, institutional records and personal archives, but there are some preliminary comments that may be useful before we look at each of these in detail.

Official documents are held in national and local archives specially established for the purpose. Scott points out that these comprise simply 'the single largest class of documents available to the social researcher' (Scott 1990, p. 16). They contain, as one would expect, a great deal of material directly related to administration and policy, involving the general maintenance of affairs as well as the day-to-day discussion of issues and problems. However, they include not only committee papers and memoranda but also letters from the public, records of interviews with interest groups, clippings from newspaper reports and notes on particular institutions. That is to say, not only are they relevant to public or official concerns at a national level, but they may also be highly significant for research on communities, neighbourhoods, institutions, families and individuals.

Institutional records may be retained by the institution itself, or else passed on to a repository such as a local record office or a university. They include interest groups and political parties, businesses, churches, clubs, societies and trade unions, and organisations such as schools, universities, hospitals, libraries, factories, prisons and retail outlets. They may have a range of types of documents. Such records may include evidence of public dealings and the attentions of the State, but they may also reveal much about the inner workings of the organisation itself, or about its employees and clients.

Similarly, personal archives may be encountered in the residence of the individual concerned, perhaps stored informally in the attic or in a trunk in the cellar, which for full access may be passed on to an established record centre. Again, these can encompass a wide range of types of documents. They are most likely to reveal aspects of the personal life of the individual and perhaps about their family and work, but in many cases they can also illuminate issues relating to the local community or to broader social and political concerns. Often, individuals involved in a particular society, or in a national committee or other association, may have retained relevant records for their own use, and these can be very useful complementary sources for researchers who are primarily interested in these institutions.

Thus, each of these types of archival collections can transcend simple and straightforward typologies of 'public' and 'private'. This means that researchers can find significant material relating to their own interests in the most unexpected of locations. Such collections may also have something to offer both to the past and to the present. In the case of official documents in particular there are important limitations in this respect, as in many (but not all) countries there are restrictions on access to recent and contemporary records. However, it may still be possible to negotiate access in such instances. In relation to institutional and personal records, these restrictions are often much less marked, and one may be able to locate a large amount of documentary material dealing with current topics and problems.

The key to any archive is its catalogue or inventory, which should specify every document or set of documents held in the collection and a code for ordering document files for use. It may be necessary to visit the archive in order to consult the catalogue, but it has become increasingly common for the catalogue to be accessible online so that researchers can have at least some sense of what is included before making what may be a long and expensive journey. The British Public Record Office, for example, has an online catalogue, PROCAT, that has transformed the nature of the subject search (see http://www.pro.gov.uk). This provides a general description of each document rather than details of its contents, but can indicate where to find any specific subject in the archive. As Amanda Bevan enthuses in her guide to tracing ancestors at the Public Record Office, 'PROCAT makes searching the whole collection of over 8.5 million records, the work of a moment. You can search by word, date, within all of the catalogue or within a part of the catalogue with incredible ease' (Bevan 2002, p. 12). Nevertheless, the catalogue can be misleading. Relevant documents can often be included in a file which is mainly on a different topic, and so a wide range of files needs to be checked. Also, a file that seems from the catalogue description to be highly promising for your research may glean very little.

For example, Gillian Sutherland has recalled making use of the establishment or personnel files of the education service in nineteenth-century England at the Public Record Office in London: 'They are virtually non-existent: only Matthew Arnold's survives. "Ah," you think, "at last." So you send for ED 36/1 and find it entirely consists of letters asking when can he take his holidays.' However, Sutherland continues, the Treasury establishment files do include some valuable records on education personnel:

> One suspects that the Treasury kept everything in case somebody at some point was going to sue them. Those groups of files relating to the Education Department at T1 and T9 are a mine of information on establishment policy, which in turn becomes a central issue of education policy in general, because the particular grant system is actually very expensive in terms of personnel to administer. These do much to compensate for the gaps in the departmental files.
>
> (Sutherland 1981, p. 80)

This highlights the need to be flexible when consulting an archival source, and to be alert for material hidden away in files whose relevance is less than obvious. It also suggests that researchers should be aware of the potential relevance of more than one government department. In relation to education, for instance, as Gosden points out, the files of the Treasury, the Department of the Environment and the Department of Employment are all significant sources (Gosden 1981; see also Morton 1997 for a guide to education-related records at the British Public Record Office).

When one travels to an archive to consult documents for the purposes of research it is difficult to know in advance how much time to allow. One may be hopeful of completing the task in one working day but find that it may take weeks, or vice versa. Where possible it can be useful to make a preliminary visit as a scouting mission, so to speak, to gain a clearer sense of what will be involved. Even this may not always give a full picture. For example, some files will be very bulky and include a great deal of relevant material, while others will have very little in them that is of any relevance. On the one hand, I have often had to work through a single file of documents for two weeks or even more, while on the other it may be possible to scan the contents of twenty files or more within a single day. Moreover, archives vary greatly as to the time taken to order and receive files of documents. In some cases, including most documents held at the Public Record Office, one will receive the files within an hour of ordering them, although usually only a limited number can be ordered at any one time, so this itself needs to be planned carefully. In others, documents may be delivered to the researcher only once or twice a day at set times, or they may be brought from another site which may take a day or more, and so the research needs to be organised with this in mind. The inherent frustrations of such research, eloquently articulated by Steedman (2001) as we have already seen, stem partly from this basic unpredictability, including the time spent waiting for orders to arrive which then may have little of value.

Archives are also highly conscious of security as the guardians of original documents which in most cases are unique and cannot be replaced. This means that the researcher is obliged to follow strict procedures in order to carry out their work. Bags are often checked before entering the archive, and in some cases are not allowed inside at all, and when leaving there may be further checks to make sure that no documents have been taken. Usually only pencils and not pens are allowed for the purposes of taking notes, in order to minimise the danger of damaging or defacing the documents in use. Manual transcription may be the only method allowed, especially where the documents are fragile and deemed to be of special value; and when photocopying is permitted it is often very expensive. The conditions of access to the documents may also include an agreement to seek permission to quote particular sections before including them in a book, article or thesis. In such cases, it is especially important to keep a copy of the conditions of access carefully and to follow these procedures as required. Extensive paraphrasing or description of documents which one is not allowed to quote directly may also be a sensitive issue that should be approached carefully.

Official documents

Official documents are generally housed in national archives or record offices specially created and maintained to store, protect and provide access to them in secure conditions. Modern archives developed from the eighteenth century to embody the nation-state and to provide a record of its administration. As such, as Steedman suggests, they 'came into being in order to solidify and memorialise first monarchical and then state power' (Steedman 1999, p. 67). This legacy is significant in helping us to understand the nature of such collections. According to Steedman, indeed, 'in its quiet folders and bundles is the neatest demonstration of how state power has operated, through ledgers and lists and indictments, and through what is missing from them' (Steedman 1999, p. 67). Other aspects of the historical formation of national archives are also worthy of note. First, they became established broadly at the same time that modern notions of 'public' and 'private' were being developed, the former around affairs of state, the latter around individuals and families, in which ideals of citizenship and society became divorced from those of the State. Secondly, and related to this, they reflected a male domination of the public sphere, establishing what have been recently described as 'spaces reserved mostly for professional men' (Smith 1998, p. 105). Nor were they remote from the 'science of freedom' characterised by the Enlightenment of the late eighteenth century (Gay 1970), but an invention that lent itself to the modern pursuit of knowledge.

Monarchical collections were established for example by Charles V of Spain (the Archivo de Simancas) in 1542, and by James I of England in 1610 (Tyacke 2001, p. 12). The first avowedly national archive was created in France in 1789, a product of the French Revolution. At first this new departure threatened to be the instrument of the destruction of the records of the *ancien régime*, but this temptation was resisted, and the Archives Départmentales established in 1796 provided for the first time a unified and comprehensive administration of public records (*Encyclopaedia Britannica* 1974). Other national archives followed, and were joined also by local and regional centres. In the United States the National Archives were established in 1930, and the Federal Records Act of 1950 authorised the creation of regional records repositories.

The development of the national archive in Britain provides an interesting case study of expanding access but continuing restrictions. The Public Record Office (PRO) was established under the Public Record Office Act of 1838, primarily to bring together the records of the Exchequer, Chancery and other ancient courts of law into a single repository. A purpose-built repository and reading room were created in Chancery Lane, London, in 1858. In the twentieth century, as the volume of records and demands on them grew, the administration of the national archive was reformed under the Public Records Act of 1958 (for further details of the PRO's development to this point see Cantwell 1991). Since April 2003 the PRO has come together with the Historical Manuscripts Commission, which following its foundation in 1869 has been responsible for other archives and manuscripts, to form the National Archives (web address at www.nationalarchives. gov.uk). Records were open to all members of the public, but remained closed to public inspection for fifty years under the 1958 Act, reduced to thirty under a further Act in 1967. This so-called 'Thirty Year Rule' included further restrictions to researchers, for example in exempting some records on grounds of national security or in cases of special sensitivity, and in its application only from the date of the closing of the relevant file in the government department concerned as opposed to the date of particular documents (see also, for example, Cox 1990).

These restrictions have often limited my own ability to research recent and contemporary issues that were not particularly sensitive. In the 1980s, when I was researching the development of secondary technical schools in England from the 1940s to the 1960s, I was unable to gain access to official records dating later than 1958. Even some materials from before this date were inaccessible because they were included in files that held some later documents. Thus, for example, I was not able to gain access to the files of the Crowther committee, which was established in 1956 to examine the education of boys and girls between fifteen and eighteen years of age, but did not report until the end of 1959 (Ministry of Education 1959). I was interested in the similarities and differences between the secondary technical schools and contemporary initiatives such as the Technical and Vocational Education Initiative and the city technology colleges, but was unable to use official records for this purpose (see McCulloch 1989).

The former rigidity of the British Thirty Year Rule has been relaxed to some extent, and the Freedom of Information Act, in force from 2005, establishes a more general right of access to information held by public authorities. Greater freedom to make use of contemporary records is potentially of major significance for educational and social researchers. However, there is still a long way to go before official records in Britain can be researched in a similar way to those in some other countries. In Sweden, under the Freedom of the Press Act originally introduced in 1766, the records of public administrations can be made public almost immediately (Tyacke 2001, p. 9). In New Zealand, where I also consulted official records in the 1980s, I was able to make use of very recent files, in some cases only a few months old. This made it possible for me to examine the nature of effects of contemporary education policies in a way that has been very difficult in Britain. My research on secondary school catchment areas or 'zoning' in New Zealand was a product of this very different research regime. I could trace the origins and development of school zoning policy from these archival sources, and also examine the contemporary nature and implications of what had become a highly controversial area of policy (see for example McCulloch 1990, 1991a). Departmental civil servants who were responsible for developing the policy attended seminars and read papers in which I presented this work, and this was hopefully of some use in helping to inform policy decisions.

Case study 3 is an example of this kind of official document, consulted at the New Zealand National Archive in Wellington. It is drawn from the records of the Education Department concerned with secondary education in particular, and enrolment schemes in particular. It is not a memorandum or committee paper, although there are many of those, but a letter from a parent to the new Minister of Education, Russell Marshall, in the Labour government that was elected to office in 1984. Because of the potential sensitivities of the case I have altered the names of the family involved and also of the locations and schools, which were in a large urban area in the North Island.

Case Study 3

New Zealand National Archive, Wellington
Education Department records
File number: 34/1/3/1 Part 9: Secondary education – general – secondary schools enrolment schemes

Mrs N. Ota to Russell Marshall (Minister of Education), 27 September 1984

I am writing to you in desperation and as a last resort to get my son into the Secondary School of our choice and his.

Both his sister and brother went to A High School and I never had any trouble with either of them. I found the discipline at A much better than our local school. We are about five streets out of zone and I think the Headmaster is using this as an excuse in turning my son down, for A High.

My husband is recovering from major surgery for cancer and I myself am not well, I am a diabetic, and also I'm on nerve tablets as I'm a nervous wreck, and worrying about my son's education is not helping any of us.

continued on facing page

The reason we do not wish our son to attend B College is a big percentage of the pupils are glue sniffers also they smoke on the way home from school and I have seen a number of them at the B Town Centre during school hours playing on the Space Invaders machine. My son went to the Town Centre after school to get my medicine from the chemist and he was bailed up by about 20 Maori and Pacific Island pupils from B College whose names we didn't know so we couldn't do anything about it, this is the main reason he won't go to the B College next year, he is petrified as he is a very sensitive boy and is not used to gangs and fighting. He got a good report from C Intermediate and a 3 + for his overall effort.

The only other way out I can see is to sell up our family home where we have lived for 24 years, or else send John away to live with someone who is living in the A area, although I know that either of these suggestions would upset John more than he already is. I do hope you will be able to help our situation as I have been ill with Migraine and Nausea since I received the letter back from A High.

After consulting on the case the Minister wrote back to this parent on 23 October 1984 to explain that unfortunately he could not help, because A High School could accept only a maximum of fifteen children from the area of B College, which had already been taken. Such episodes demonstrate the potential value of official records as a source for educational and social researchers. They also emphasise the important point that these records not only are useful for an understanding of administration and policy matters, but can reflect the interactions between the State and individuals, families and social institutions.

In many countries, local official records are housed separately from those of the central administration and departments, and researchers are able to consult them in different locations although under similar conditions. These can also shed light on the workings of the central State because they include discussions with civil servants and politicians on particular issues, as well as providing material on the concerns of local people on a range of topics. For example, in New Zealand I was able to consult files held at the Northern Regional Office of the Department of Education in Auckland. Two of these files, 26/1/88 and 26/1/89, constituted the papers of an investigating committee established in 1970 to look into the growth of juvenile gangs in the city of Auckland. This included representatives from different departments, the police, social workers and welfare officers. File 26/1/88 turned out to contain a full set of the minutes of the committee, while 26/1/89 included correspondence, reports and memoranda brought to its attention leading to a final report issued in October 1970. The committee minutes are detailed, and bring out key issues raised in the discussion as well as their conclusions. For example, on 23 September 1970 the committee met to review progress made before finalising its report. Under the heading 'General Leadership in the Community', the following points are recorded (actual names changed or coded by myself):

> The Secretary reported on his discussions with the Headmasters of A Primary, B Primary and C College. The general consensus was that they didn't have any staff who would live in the community under present conditions. It was felt that if attractive financial concessions were made or if housing similar to school houses in country service schools were available it would do much to attract leadership in the community from amongst the teaching profession. Mr Smith [Inspector of Schools] said that the situation in regard to staffing inadequacies was known to his Department. The desirability of police living in the community was discussed. It was considered desirable to have policemen closely identified with the community but Sergeant Jones [Police and Youth Aid] made the point that the demands on a resident officer would be unreasonable and the average policeman wouldn't want to live in the area.

A further discussion of gang activity in primary and intermediate schools is recorded, followed by comments on the exploitation of gangs:

> Inspector Brown stated that gangs were not being used for political purposes. Mr Green [Regional Controller, Maori Welfare, and the committee chairman] felt that there was some quasi political agitation and anti-pakeha [European] feeling. He felt that some gang members came back from Borstal more radical and aggressive. Mr Orange [District Probation Officer] felt that the authority of elders was being undermined and that members who aligned or were in contact with the educated were being menaced by other gang members. Mr Purple [District Child Welfare Officer] also commented that good influences were being forced out.

The meeting then discussed a tentative foreword to the Report and noted some further suggestions and submissions by local interests.

The same file also includes notes taken by a member of the committee, Mr Scott (Youth Activities Officer), on the discussion held at the meeting of 23 September. These acknowledged the various areas of opinion, but suggested that there was one common factor involved, educational problems, and that therefore the solution needed to involve a new approach to education:

ONE COMMON FACTOR.

Lack of success at school academically/recreationally, therefore lack of happiness at school academically/recreationally.

Led to rejection of authority at early age and consequent acceptance of anti-social, anti-establishment attitudes. Expression in gangs as compensation to fill in idle hours.

Must start with changes in school system – language problems – social education – recreation – trade training = Education for living with continuity into adolescence and adulthood.

Schools as com. Centres.

Technical institutes for evening classes (already done) also other training centres.

Extra curricular activities (Soc. Rec.) after normal school hours.

Encouragement in Primary School and hobbies.

Culture (Drama, Music, Dance) pastimes and sports.

Employment of trained supervisors.

Must deal with this unique Auckland situation.

Maoris to town – influx of Islanders.

1st generation urban dwellers. All with special needs and problems.

Department policy to involve Local Bodies. Local Bodies may be reluctant to accept this expensive liability. We must stress urgency and not allow issue to become bogged down in political procedures.

Education before coming to City/N.Z.

This emphasis on education is reflected also in the committee's final report, a draft of which is included in the accompanying file, 26/1/89. It is notable that the recommendations of the report in the area of education are very similar to the advice of a memorandum submitted by the Department of Education, also in file 26/1/89. This focused on the needs of Maori and Pacific Island children, rather than of pakeha or European pupils, and included proposals on pre-school education, curriculum and staffing, and pre-vocational and vocational training. In relation to the latter, the Department suggested that schooling for 'middle and slower groups of Maori and Island pupils' should be made 'more realistic to them and their parents' through a greater emphasis on vocational guidance and employment skills. The draft copy of the committee's report refers to the need for a more 'realistic' type of course at secondary school. In fact, in this copy the word 'vocational' in deleted in favour of 'realistic'. This is remarkably similar to the approach adopted by the Newsom committee on average and below-average children of thirteen to sixteen years of age in Britain in the early 1960s, the papers of which are in the Ministry of Education files in the Public Record Office, London (meeting files ED.146/45 and ED.145/46, Public Record Office; final report published as Ministry of Education 1963a; see also McCulloch 1998, especially chapter 8). In the latter case, an early draft suggested that 'Most of our boys are going to work with their hands, whether in skilled or unskilled jobs', but after protests by some members of the committee 'most' was replaced with the word 'many' (Ministry of Education papers, Public Record Office, London, file ED.146/45).

A number of points may be made in reflecting on the use of these committee minutes and papers. They do reveal a great deal about the discussion of the issues and how the debate developed, and help to take the educational and social researcher behind the scenes to what are in many cases frank and open commentaries, as opposed to the coded and often cautious public sources. Contributions to the committee discussion were also careful in their use of terms, but often more willing to use direct references to issues rather than veiling them, for example in talking about 'vocational' as opposed to 'realistic' approaches to the curriculum. These papers also illuminate the connections between a range of public and social services in dealing with specific issues, including significant links for example between educational authorities and police, social work, child welfare and housing. Another notable point is that the committee minutes, while full and revealing on a number of interests and views, give an emphasis to a developing consensus and especially to the comments of the chairman. This indeed is similar to the tendency in the British Cabinet minutes quoted in the last chapter. Moreover, they give the impression of a logical and sequential discussion whereas in many cases the debate in the meeting itself may well have been much less coherent. In other cases, much less discussion is recorded in the minutes, but it is still important for the researcher to take careful note of such details as who was present, interests represented, date, and venue. It may be possible to find out what was actually going on at the meeting from other sources, including the records of individuals who took part.

The report produced in this instance is also instructive as an example of a useful approach to understanding policy reports in general. This is based not simply on a reading of the final version as published, but on tracing the processes involved in their construction. Consulting the records of the committee will reveal the underlying assumptions and aims of the committee in a way that the final approved, careful text may not. It will also provide significant insights into contestation between different interests represented on the committee or in relation to government or community pressures. Such opportunities for researchers can also be found in the records of interest groups and individuals involved in these committees, as seen below.

Institutional records

Alongside the records and archives of nation-states there has also grown an abundance of material generated by a wide range of social institutions. As interest has increased in the development of social, cultural and economic agencies, so these have often taken special care to preserve their records for the use of researchers. In many cases these have been kept in-house, sometimes in difficult working conditions, so that the institution can itself continue to make use of them. Otherwise they may be donated to universities for safe keeping and to catalogue, maintain and provide access. Often a large number of different collections may be housed in a particular university.

For example, at the University of Warwick near Coventry, England, a Modern Records Centre (MRC) was opened in 1973, with the intention of attracting records to support the study of new forms of social history, especially labour history. It was felt that these had been generally neglected, and that a sustained effort was necessary to locate and preserve this kind of source material. In many cases it was found that such records either did not exist or had not survived, but a major repository was soon developed especially for trade unions and industrial relations (Storey 1978). Thirty years later, the MRC had many hundreds of collections, large and small, most notably for trade unions and similar organisations, employers' and trades associations and industrial relations, but also for more general pressure groups, political parties and organisations, business and management, individuals, education and miscellaneous records.

One major collection held at the MRC is that of the Trades Union Congress (TUC) (MSS. 292), a voluntary association of trade unions originally formed in Manchester in 1868, and now the largest pressure group in Britain. This consists mainly of the files of the TUC's central registry from 1920 to 1991, including correspondence, internal and external documents, minutes, reports, printed material and press statements. The extent of the collection is 160.56 cubic metres and there are no restrictions on access for researchers. The involvement of the TUC in a wide range of national and local organisations, and also in political affairs especially in relation to the Labour Party and central government, ensures that this collection is highly significant for social researchers. In specific areas such as education the TUC collection holds records of considerable importance, for example the minutes of the TUC's education committee, evidence submitted to the Board of Education consultative committee and later the Central Advisory Council of the Ministry of Education on a range of issues, correspondence on matters as diverse as the school leaving age, young workers, maintenance allowances, corporal punishment and citizenship (see also http:// modernrecords.warwick.ac.uk/sumguide.shtml for further details on this collection and others held at the MRC in Warwick).

Another English university, the University of Leeds, has acquired over the years a number of archival collections with particular relevance to education. Among these is the archive of the Association of Education Committees, which represented local education authorities at a national level in England and Wales from 1904 until 1977. Upon its demise, it donated its archive of about four thousand files of minute books, papers and correspondence to the University of Leeds to provide a resource that would be available to researchers concerned with the use of educational planning and administration (Gosden 1981, p. 91). Some of these are valuable for the light that they shed on changes in national policy, such as for example file A511 on the Curriculum Study Group (CSG) established by the Ministry of Education in 1962, and a large number of files concerned with the Schools Council for Curriculum and Examinations in the 1960s and 1970s. File A511 features a classic exchange between Dame Mary Smieton, permanent secretary of the Ministry of Education, and Sir William Alexander, the long-serving secretary of the AEC, on the role of the State in curricular issues. In a letter to Alexander dated 9 March 1962, Smieton sought to justify the establishment of the CSG in the following terms:

> The main job of the unit will be to improve the value of the service that the Inspectorate and the Department have for a long time sought to offer in the field of curriculum and examinations . . . In other words, our aim will be to offer a service, for those who want to use it, and to provide a chopping block for those who find stimulation for their own thinking in reacting against the findings of others working in the same field. But we have no intention of disturbing in any way the present pattern of powers and responsibilities, in the area of curriculum and examinations, and we shall constantly seek to ensure that the voice of the new unit is heard only as one voice amongst others, invested with no greater authority than is merited by the quality of its contribution to the general store of knowledge and experience.

Smieton continued in her letter:

> I believe that you will welcome this new move on our part. At a time characterised above all by the speed of change, we believe that the Ministry and Inspectorate have a useful contribution to make to thinking about the educational process, arising partly from the knowledge we obtain from the view we have of the whole of the educational field, partly from our contacts, through central government, with some of the mainsprings of change, and partly from our opportunity (which we share with some large local authorities) to form inter-disciplinary teams capable of bringing to bear on current and future problems a considerable concentration of skill and experience. And it seems to us particularly important that we should make this contribution where it is a matter – as it so often is to-day – of foreseeing changes before they become apparent on the ground, and of placing before our partners in the education service a range of possible solutions to future problems. If we can do this job, and do it well, we believe that the free-

dom of the teachers, and of the local education authorities, to take in good time the decisions which are properly theirs, will be substantially enlarged; this is our sole aim and purpose in putting the services of the new unit at the disposal of our partners.

Alexander was not convinced, as he made clear in his reply, dated 12 March:

I share your view that the speed of change in these days makes it essential that all of us should collaborate to secure the most effective means of making information available on which judgements can be made and I certainly accept that the Ministry have an important contribution to make. At the same time, I am deeply convinced of the virtue of distribution of power and of the importance of procedure by agreement. It is this basic approach which I believe makes the English pattern of education unique and, to a very large extent, the envy of the world. It may be, and indeed sometimes undoubtedly is, true that it is apparently less efficient than other procedures, but in the long-term I believe it is the most effective.

In this correspondence we see, beneath the surface veneer of politeness and consensus, a basic argument being played out as to the role of the State and the position of local interests and professionals. In fact in this case the Ministry soon made a tactical withdrawal, and abandoned the CSG in favour of the Schools Council, which was designed to represent teacher and local authority interests (see for example McCulloch 2000b). It is important also to emphasise that these policy debates and issues can be traced in the archives of societies and associations which may be located in a wide range of repositories, as in this case, and not only in national archives and local record offices.

In many other instances, records are retained – or not, as the case may be – within the institution itself. Practices of retention and destruction of records are highly varied in different institutions. Especially when the institution changes location, or develops a different function, or loses key personnel, or faces growing demands on space, the records of its previous development often appear to be luxury items that can be easily discarded. In other cases, records may be left to rot disregarded in a cupboard or basement. Even in many well established and prominent institutions it is not unusual to find that there is little or no archival material that has survived. In some cases, even though there may be a commitment on the part of current staff members to preserve such records, material is patchy because of the haphazard or careless practices of their predecessors.

In the case of schools, for example, there is a huge range of approaches to the retention and storage of records. In Britain, I have sought access to the records of many schools of different types, and have often been disappointed. Some very well known schools with long histories have retained very little. Others are loath to allow access to independent researchers. On the other hand, there are schools with extensive and useful documentary material and excellent facilities for researchers, and these may easily be recently established institutions with heavy demands on their time and space. The example of Wales High School in Rotherham in South Yorkshire, England, is interesting and instructive in this respect. This secondary school was originally established in 1970, and since that time it has stayed in the same buildings and has had only two head teachers. This stability over time has allowed it to keep most if not all of its records, amounting to hundreds of files, which have been brought together into a single collection, stored in suitable conditions, and catalogued in consultation with myself. These include the formal records of meetings of the governing body, but also many files on everyday issues affecting the development of the school.

One interesting file in the Wales High School repository is File 73, concerned with the response of the school to a major national initiative, the Technical and Vocational Education Initiative (TVEI), between 1988 and 1992. This includes a detailed report of an 'Inset Day' for staff development that was devoted to the TVEI on Tuesday 7 March 1989. There are summaries of several group discussions of teachers held during the day that reflect the anxieties of practitioners over the effects of continual policy changes. Under the topic of 'Coping with change', one group, Group E, complained that there were too many changes with too little consultation, and concluded:

> Change in itself is not the problem so far as coping is concerned, however change should not be just for the sake of change; existing practice has for the most part been successful for a long time. The concern is in the pace of change. There is need for periods of stability between changes to allow for consolidation and fine-tuning. The various changes such as GCSE [General Certificate of Secondary Education], RoA [Records of Achievement], TVEI, National Curriculum supposedly complement each other – we would like to see more evidence.

Another group, Group I, lamented:

> There is an increasing input of new initiatives in our profession, which overlay the previous initiatives which we are still trying to successfully cope with. The changes are imposed from outside agencies and the teaching staff have little opportunity to modify or shape these changes. They therefore tend to be viewed as an imposition rather than as progressive development and this reduces the motivation of staff to greet the change with real enthusiasm. The general impression given to the

public about teachers is that they are overpaid and under-worked and this further depresses the staff's motivation to be creative. The rate of change is such that the massive effort put in by staff members to produce materials for new courses is wasted when a new development is rushed in without thought of continuity.

Group J had similar worries:

> At what cost? was the question then discussed. There seemed to be varying opinions from what had been learned from the morning sessions. Some had heard that one merely had to put in a justification as to why the money was needed and the use to which it would be put. All agreed this was reasonable. But then some had the impression that that was all there was to it, apart from filling in the odd progress report or so over the years; while others felt it had been stressed that there would be all sorts of paperwork to be done, 'cluster' meetings to attend, 'overseers' coming in every half-term or so to 'monitor' progress and require outline or detailed plans for the next move, etc. In other words to apply for the money was to open the floodgates to yet more 'hassle' in an already edgy and overworked profession, simply because teachers cannot be trusted to use the money well according to their professional judgment. 'Accountability' seems to mean just this, when this long and trendy word is analysed.

Matters of concern raised by staff at the end of the day's discussions included the following:

> We were told many things that TVEI was NOT . . . but the impression was given that the 'experts' are reluctant to define its boundaries and implications; perhaps they are not all that sure. From the information given it appears that we already cover a large number of the aspects which make up TVEI schemes; is TVEI, therefore, relevant and appropriate to Wales? The impression was given that other schools had manipulated their applications for financial support in order to get the cash – somewhat immoral, if not distasteful.

> Concern expressed over our inability to shake off the feeling in TVEI of *industry*/work/training/functionalism with the consequent lack of concern for *education*. There seemed to be an emphasis on 'narrow' training for roles in production/industry. Good schools do, in any case, review their methodology for active learning. Why TVEI? So far TVEI has involved schools in starting new courses NOT 'developing'. *Why* involve TVEI in 'becoming better'/building on what we do now? Can

> TVEI help with extra staffing? Timetabling? There is considerable scepticism about TVEI itself and its philosophy.
>
> The morning session was baffling for some staff; they are no clearer as to how to implement the scheme in their individual departments. Guidance is necessary in places but yet each school is different. Most staff are tied to 35 [teaching] periods per week and have little time to develop initiatives like TVEI.

These concerns also reflected the scepticism of the then head teacher of the school, which may help to explain why they were so freely expressed and recorded.

These and similar documents drawn from the Wales High School documents are significant in a number of ways. They suggest the scope that exists for discerning the attitudes and everyday practices of members of ordinary local institutions who might variously be described as employees, practitioners or professionals. They also show potential differences between the official doctrines expressed in policy initiatives and the often unexpected and confused responses to them, albeit that the doubts raised here are all from a single institution. Moreover, they help to reveal changes in approach that have played themselves out over time. In this respect, it is helpful to compare the frustrations experienced by these teachers at Wales High School in 1989 with the debate in 1962 between the Ministry of Education official and the local authority representative, as quoted above. They seem to betoken an underlying development in the active intervention of the State in the curriculum that contradicts the bland official assurances. As in other cases, then, here we see an interesting example of interaction between the State, social institutions and professional identities. Moreover, both the particular example of Wales High School and the changes over the medium term may be pursued through research that need not involve travelling to the Public Record Office, or that treats the national archive as a complementary or subsidiary source.

Personal archives

In the case of personal archives, again there are many of these to be found in a wide range of repositories. Such archives vary greatly in their size and nature. Some individuals have taken care to retain every significant item about their life, and often many insignificant ones as well, and have had these transferred in good condition to a recognised archive. Others, including many who have been highly prominent in their life and work, have left very little. In some cases the material amassed by individuals during their lifetime has been destroyed or lost after their death, sometimes for reasons of sensitivity or because of lack of space or care.

One fascinating example of an extensive personal archive is that of Marie Stopes, a leading twentieth-century British campaigner for sexual freedom. Stopes retained nearly all of her papers and correspondence, and after her death in 1958 nearly three tons of material arrived at the British Library in London for sorting. Sixty archival boxes containing over three hundred files are held in the Contemporary Medical Archives Centre at the Wellcome Institute for the History of Medicine in London. In particular, these include her correspondence on sexual problems with men and women around the world. Lesley A. Hall, who has researched these papers in depth, notes that the letters sent to Stopes survive in abundance, in many cases together with carbon copies of her replies or notes for her secretaries. As Hall suggests,

> This mass of correspondence forms a rich and unique source for the study of sexual ideas and attitudes in the 1920s and 1930s in particular (the period during which her popularity was at its height). It demonstrates the immense impact her works had on those who read them, and the questions raised in their minds to which they sought further answers.
>
> (Hall 1991, p. 10)

Hall also notes that the letters in this collection 'open up an undiscovered world of suffering and emotion' that far from being atypical or unrepresentative may well constitute 'the tip of an iceberg' (Hall 1991, p. 12). In this way, Hall contends, they comprise evidence that contradicts the orthodox and respectable views on sex usually found in textbooks and official reports.

Another very large personal archive is that of the former New Zealand Prime Minister Sir Walter Nash, who died in 1968. According to his biographer, Keith Sinclair, Nash amassed the most extensive collection of private papers ever known in New Zealand. It occupied a study and a very large garage, constituting over three thousand bundles and boxes of documents. Even when newspapers and journals were removed from the collection it still weighed several tons, and it took up 700 feet of shelves when it was moved to the National Archives. The collection includes many letters from other Labour leaders, and also many documents involving politicians, economists, public servants, academics, parsons and public figures. Sinclair notes that, even when he was a Cabinet minister, Nash kept his own copies of correspondence on any topics he thought to be important, which meant that it was unnecessary to look at the different departmental files in the National Archives. On the other hand, Sinclair did need to make supplementary visits to the Public Record Office in London and to the Franklin Roosevelt papers in the United States in order to discern British and American attitudes to negotiations involving Nash. 'Many people have asked how I could stand reading all these documents,' commented Sinclair, 'but historians will understand their fascination' (Sinclair 1976, p. v).

In my own research, I have often found personal archives to be of great value in illuminating individual contributions to public issues, and as a source that can provide important material on events and problems to which the person involved was a witness. For example, Professor Sydney Raybould, a professor of adult education at the University of Leeds in the 1950s, left a fairly small collection of papers after his death that was housed in the Museum of the History of Education at the University of Leeds. While working on some other material in the Museum as a researcher at the University of Leeds in the early 1980s, I decided out of curiosity to have a look at the Raybould collection. When I did so, I found to my astonishment that it included a full set of minutes and memoranda on the Crowther committee on education for fifteen- to eighteen-year-olds, of which he was a member. As I have already noted earlier in this chapter, this material was not fully available in the official records at the Public Record Office for another ten years, but I was able to use it without restrictions at my own university. Among the papers in the Raybould collection were memoranda by the Chairman, the Assessor and various members of the Crowther committee of the 1950s on different aspects of the problem being studied. These included statistical surveys, notes on meetings of sub-groups, and reports on conferences and publications on related issues. Box 10 of the collection included copies of memoranda from forty-three associations supplying evidence to the committee. Correspondence between members of the committee also reflects different views about what to include in the final Report, and the nature of the processes involved in the inquiry. As a whole, this collection was most important for my own study of secondary technical education in the 1950s as a complementary source to the evidence available at the Public Record Office. As with national and institutional collections, therefore, personal archives can be highly significant for the detailed insights that they allow into the processes taking place behind the scenes.

Another example from my own experience may help to underline the connections to be drawn between personal difficulties, professional lives and public and policy issues. This case arose from my interest in the background to the Norwood Report on the curriculum and examinations in secondary schools, published in Britain in 1943 at a key moment in the educational reform debate that culminated in the Education Act of 1944 (Board of Education 1943a; see also McCulloch 1994). I was aware that the Chairman of the committee that produced this highly controversial Report was Sir Cyril Norwood, who had been a leading figure in the educational policy community for the previous quarter of a century, but whose personal papers appeared to have vanished without trace. I set about trying to locate his surviving family, and eventually came across one of his granddaughters, Sarah Canning, who ran a small private girls' school in Dorset, England. I made the journey to Dorset highly uncertain whether there would be any material of significance for researchers. When I arrived, Miss Canning showed me to a large wooden trunk which turned out to contain a large collection of papers left by Norwood. These included background papers on the Norwood Report, a large number of press cuttings on the many issues of educational controversy during Norwood's career, drafts of sermons and speeches given by Norwood, diaries on overseas journeys, photographs, and hundreds of personal letters between himself and his then fiancée, Catherine, in the later 1890s. Together, these papers were vital in illuminating not only the development of Norwood's own life and career but also the nature of his contribution to public policy. A few years later, Norwood's surviving family decided to donate this collection to the University of Sheffield, where the materials were catalogued (Ms 230) and included in the National Register of Archives (NRA 9951).

Among the most interesting and poignant documents in the Norwood collection is a paper in the handwriting of himself and of Catherine, his wife, undated, but in fact written in 1933. This paper sets out reasons for Norwood staying as Head of the leading public school Harrow, where he had been since 1926, or leaving to accept an appointment as President of his old Oxford college, St John's. It makes clear that he had had a difficult experience at Harrow compared with his previous posts as Head Master of Bristol Grammar School (1906–16) and Master of Marlborough College (1917–26), and also that Catherine was most unhappy there. At the same time, it reveals the mixed emotions involved in abandoning the service to which he was committed and in thinking about the kinds of contributions that might be possible in the future. Among the reasons Norwood put forward for staying were:

> I do not believe that as President of a College it is possible for me to make any direct impact on undergraduate life. It is more likely to lead to official business e.g. statutes, investments, general policy. This does not attract me much.

> I may, and probably shall, be thought of as having really been beaten by Harrow. Yet I know that I have now practically the whole staff with me, and the boys trusting me.

> Harrow would regard it as a disaster, and I have reason to be grateful to many.

Reasons for leaving included:

It provides for the next 12 years, and probably 17, if health and strength are given, a position of comfort and dignity with abundant leisure.

My wife hates Harrow, and regards another 7 years with dread . . .

I too am an 'alien' at Harrow. It has never been a part of me as Bristol and Marlborough were. It is probable therefore that another man would serve Harrow better because he could love it more.

Catherine's responses to these points, added to the same document, are even more personal in tone. She points out that if they left Harrow, 'there is a chance of her making something out of her last years of life – at least she could not run a boarding house for other people. She might be able to be of some use to somebody and not the drone she is here, whose one object is to try and fill her time up and pass away the hours.' She added:

Looking back on the last seven years it is the hurt to ourselves which it is difficult to forgive Harrow for – but if you feel that you are not going to be happy, I will again try to do all I can to make things as easy as I can for you and to help you even if it is only by running the house and being of use when and where I can be – but I will try loyally to do my best which ever way you decide. I will try and not fail you at the end of our 30 years partnership.

Finally, she dismissed with some force Norwood's reference to colleagues at Harrow to whom he was grateful: 'To whom have you to be grateful? Your staff? Friends – you have none.' Norwood accepted the appointment at St John's, Oxford, and remained there until his retirement in 1946.

This is clearly an intensely personal document, and sheds a great deal of light on both Cyril and Catherine Norwood and their long companionate relationship. It is also highly significant for the evidence that it affords on Norwood's professional life and career, and his approach to public service. He regarded himself as 'an "alien" in Harrow', and thought that someone else who might 'love it more' would serve it better. By contrast, both Bristol and Marlborough had been 'part of me'. He was anxious to find a new challenge, but not simply in 'official business', rather in an area where it would be possible to make a 'direct impact'. The loneliness and sacrifice evoked by both Cyril and Catherine in this document provide a very different perspective from the rather severe and aloof public image that Norwood generally projected. There was a vocation rather than simply a career in their contribution to education, and it was one that enmeshed both their personal and their working lives.

Overall, this chapter has given some clues to the massive resources that are available to educational and social researchers in archives and records, but that are often neglected. They can be overwhelming, inaccessible, inconvenient and intimidating. Yet this material, amassed and retained by a wide range of agencies and individuals, is of immense importance for educational and social, as for historical research. It is crucial for our understanding of the past, but is also potentially significant for contemporary research and for demonstrating the development of issues over time. Such resources are a key source of evidence on public issues, but also help to link together the public with the private. They are useful in developing connections between different aspects of society and culture. In penetrating the underlying assumptions, problems and conflicts involved in education and society, they do indeed take us a long way behind the scenes.

Suggestions for further reading

History of the Human Sciences (1998, 1999), special issues on The Archive, 11/4 and 12/2

McCulloch, G. (1989) *The Secondary Technical School: A Usable Past?*, Falmer, London

Morton, A. (1997) *Education and the State from 1833*, PRO Publications, London

Scott, J. (1990) *A Matter of Record: Documentary Sources in Social Research*, Polity, Cambridge

Steedman, C. (2001) *Dust*, Manchester University Press, Manchester

http://www.modernrecords.warwick.ac.uk/sumguide/shtml

http://www.nationalarchives.gov.uk

5 On the Record

Printed Media and Literature

The media, defined broadly, are public channels of communications (Briggs and Burke 2002). Printed media and literature constitute public source material, readily accessible to researchers. They provide public accounts and reporting of events for a broad readership. They are useful in relation to both past and present. In this chapter we will examine first of all books and their value for documentary-based studies. We will then investigate the use of official reports and proceedings, and the potential role of secondary analysis of existing datasets. Thirdly, newspapers, magazines and other periodicals will be assessed. Finally, we will discuss the significance of creative and fictional literature, such as novels, and consider to what extent this kind of work can be of use for educational, historical and social researchers. Books and reports are particularly useful as evidence on public issues or debates, while newspapers and creative literature give special purchase to everyday life and experience.

Historians often regard such material as being relatively low in the hierarchy of primary sources. Tosh suggests for example that 'In the historian's hierarchy of sources those that carry most weight are the ones that arise directly from everyday business or social intercourse, leaving open the task of interpretation' (2002, p. 59). Books, broadsheets and newspapers may offer 'valuable insights into the mentality of the age', he continues, and yet for the historian 'they are no substitute for the direct, day-to-day evidence of thought and action provided by the letter, the diary and the memorandum', which constitute 'the "records" of history *par excellence*'. Indeed, Tosh insists, public sources

> contain only what was considered to be fit for public consumption – what governments were prepared to reveal, what journalists could elicit from tight-lipped informants, what editors thought would gratify their readers, or MPs their constituents. In each case there is a controlling purpose which may limit, distort or falsify what is said.
>
> (2002, p. 65)

For this reason, according to Tosh, 'Historians wish to be as nearly as possible observers of the events in question; they do not want to deliver themselves into the hands of a narrator or commentator. The most revealing source is that which was written with no thought for posterity' (Tosh 2002, p. 59). At the same time, social researchers have become increasingly prone to take such sources for granted as types of evidence, and thus to neglect them in favour of other material. Secondary analysis of publicly available data, for example, tends to be seen merely as rehashing 'old' data (Hakim 1982, p. 1). Yet, while they are usually not difficult to find, they can be just as valuable as the most esoteric and inaccessible source.

Books

Books are a very familiar artefact, but are modern in their construction and in the early twenty-first century are increasingly under challenge from other forms of communication. They originated in their modern form with the printing press in the mid fifteenth century, and proliferated in the early sixteenth century. They brought with them the notion of an author who is solely responsible for the work, encouraged the idea of intellectual property and made possible a fixed, correct and authorised version of the text to be distributed however large the distance or community involved (Febvre and Martin 1958/1984; Briggs and Burke 2002). In the nineteenth century, new printing techniques and improved transport led to increasing numbers of books being published and a reduction in their price, which in turn consolidated their central place in the print culture (Secord 2000). Over these past five hundred years they have embodied knowledge and scholarship, and have also been a principal means of challenging established orthodoxies, even more powerful in this sense than the gunpowder and portable firearms that had been invented shortly before (Febvre and Martin 1958/1984, p. 10). Tracts and treatises are key sources of documentary evidence that reflect the arguments of a society or culture and how they develop, whether the doctrinal disputes of the sixteenth century, the conflicts over religion and science in the nineteenth century or the social and political antagonisms of our own day. This, however, does not mean that any individual work may be taken as necessarily representative of attitudes in any given context. It is also important not to assume that their readers believed what was written, still less that they put the ideas in them into practice, and so their influence must always be open to question.

One example of employing books for the study of public debates over key issues of contention relates to secondary education in Britain in the 1950s. A so-called tripartite system of grammar, technical and modern schools was established following the Education Act of 1944. Technical schools failed to develop as was envisaged, and modern schools, for the majority of secondary school pupils, did not achieve sufficient esteem with the public.

However, the grammar schools were widely recognised for their promotion of academic achievement and individual merit for the small minority of secondary school pupils who attended them. The supporters of the grammar schools attempted to capitalise on their success, as well as to forestall the possibility that they might be dismantled to allow a broader range of pupils to enjoy academic success. It was in this situation that Dr Eric James, the High Master of Manchester Grammar School, produced a book designed to promote the ideals and achievements of the grammar schools, entitled *Education and Leadership* (1951). In this work, James argued that a modern society such as Britain needed to be able to recognise and develop the characteristics of leadership. An indispensable means of doing so, James insisted, was to cultivate a recognisable and distinct elite through the education system and the schools. The social and political elite thus nurtured would be based neither on birth nor on wealth, as it had been in the past, but on talent or 'merit'. According to James, such was the historic task of the grammar schools, 'the spearhead of a social revolution no less real for being unspectacular' (James 1951, p. 38). Indeed, 'One of the most significant aspects of the educational and social history of the past fifty years has been the way in which national leadership in almost every sphere has been increasingly recruited from the products of the ordinary grammar schools.' In this way, he declared,

> Every child from Bricktown Secondary School who secures a commission, or a position in the administrative civil service, or a controlling place in industry or commerce, is a portent of an immense social change, the slow creation of an elite of merit, a transfer of power to those whose qualification wielding it is neither birth nor wealth, but talent.
>
> (James 1951, p. 38)

Because of this change, James suggested, the grammar schools could increasingly ensure not only that 'no potential leaders are overlooked in our processes of selection' but also that 'the leadership we produce is indeed enlightened' (James 1951, p. 40). In particular, he concluded, this enlightened elite should possess 'integrity, courage, judgement, stability, tact, and perseverance' (James 1951, p. 26). It was the role of the grammar schools, as he saw it, to nurture this combination of qualities (see also McCulloch 1991b, especially chapter 5).

James's book was a significant contribution to a gathering debate about the nature of secondary education that developed in Britain during the 1950s. However, James was on the losing side in this debate. Increasing criticism of the social effects of the tripartite system led to the rise of the comprehensive school, designed for all abilities and aptitudes. By the end of the 1950s, James's analysis was politically vulnerable and open to direct riposte from those who were seeking change. It was this that was provided by Michael Young in his work *The Rise of the Meritocracy*, first published in 1958. In this book, Young looks back from the year 2034 to review how society had developed on the basis of the arguments that James had put forward. For this purpose, Young coined the term 'meritocracy', that is, a society based on selection by merit. The elite is selected 'according to brains and educated according to deserts', allowing 'rule not so much by the people as by the cleverest people: not an aristocracy of birth, not a plutocracy of talent, but a true meritocracy of talent' (Young 1958, p. 21). Young documents the rise of the principle of 'selection by merit' in Britain, first in the reforms of the civil service and then in the system of mass education. With the improvement of selection methods, the principle of seniority in industry and the professions begins to yield to the principle of merit. Finally, 'the world beholds for the first time the spectacle of a brilliant class, the five per cent of the nation who know what five per cent means' (Young 1958, p. 103). But this story does not have a happy ending. The consolidation of a new elite serves to alienate those who are excluded, and leads to a rebellion in which the narrator of the book is himself killed.

The term 'meritocracy' entered the English language and has been widely used since its introduction in Young's book. More deeply, both Young and James need to be understood in terms of their contributions to a public debate over the character of education and society, in the context of the 1950s. They are valuable documentary sources in this respect, although their value may be enhanced still further when used in combination with other evidence such as government reports, archival sources and newspapers. For example, the archive of the Ministry of Education reveals the anxieties of Ministry officials who were conscious of the emerging social distinctions associated with the new secondary education. According to one senior official as early as 1946, 'Now that secondary education has been made free – only a very small fee-paying area remains – and admission or allocation is determined by qualification and not by ability to pay, no question of class distinction arises.' On the other hand, he continued, 'even though it may be admitted that class distinctions disappear, we are next confronted with the objection that by having different types of secondary school we should only be replacing social class distinctions by equally objectionable intellectual distinctions – creating an aristocracy of intellect in the Grammar Schools and putting the "runners-up" in the Secondary (Technical) Schools and "the field" in the Modern Schools' (Wood 1946: Ministry of Education papers, ED.136/787).

A potential issue in the use of such public works is that they can become over-familiar as representing debates and problems. They are often employed by social researchers and historians as a useful means of articulating attitudes or conflicts, with the result that they exaggerate the representative nature and influence of the work in question. For example, a book by G.C.T. Giles, a communist and teachers' union leader, entitled *The New School Tie* (1946), is habitually enlisted as expressing widespread opposition to the educational reforms of the 1940s. Ken Jones refers to 'the concerns of Giles and of thousands of reformers like him' being encapsulated in this work (Jones 2003, p. 16). It is important to discern the circulation and impact of works of this kind when using them as documentary sources, and also useful to widen the range of works that are employed for this purpose. Moreover, the assumptions and arguments of the authors of these works should be critically scrutinised rather than being accepted at their face value.

A particular type of book that can be useful as evidence for social researchers and historians is the textbook. These are works produced for use in schools or other educational institutions, roughly since the 1830s, when the word itself appeared (Stray 1994, p. 2), generally designed to support teachers, lecturers, pupils and students to follow a syllabus or develop it further. They have attracted attention from researchers in Europe and America, though much less so in Britain (Marsden 2001, pp. 1–3). They are highly significant not only for the way in which they present prescribed information but also for their projection of approved values and ideologies. Textbooks are indeed socially constructed artefacts that 'offer a window into the dominant values and beliefs of established groups in any given period', and act as 'gatekeepers of ideas, values and knowledge' (Foster 1999, p. 253). Apple and Christian-Smith (1991) insist that their representations of what counts as 'official knowledge' really signify deeper political, economic and cultural relations, both in the past and in the present, for example in their alignment with conservative movements. In Stray's terminology, too, they constitute 'multiply coded cultural commodities' (1994, p. 24).

Portrayals of the dissemination of social and cultural values through textbooks have underpinned a number of interesting and important studies. For example, the nature of national identity has often been examined through this device. John Ahier has discussed the ways in which national identity has been a sub-text of geography and history textbooks in Britain, including their images of the city and the countryside (Ahier 1988). Stuart Foster has investigated the treatment of ethnic groups in history textbooks in the United States in terms of a struggle for American identity. According to Foster, to understand how textbook writers in different periods of American history have responded to issues about national identity and heterogeneity is also to appreciate the dominant values and ideology of the age. It also offers 'an opportunity to appreciate how certain societal forces have validated the historical contributions of identified groups over the claims of others' (Foster 1999, pp. 251–2). Foster traces the historical development of American history textbooks to argue that they represent a white, male, Protestant middle or upper class, reflect the ingrained conservatism of

American society and have tended to endorse the capitalist system, tradi-
tional lifestyles, unquestioning patriotism and the 'Western tradition'.
Within this overall pattern he discerns shifting fashions in history textbooks
which have arisen from factors such as the changing audience. None the less,
he suggests, contemporary portrayals of American history remain nation-
alistic in tone and content, intended 'not to critically examine America's
past but to celebrate the achievements of its people' (Foster 1999, p. 267).
By contrast, he adds, they lack any deep discussion of the origins of social
inequality and poverty, and avoid attention to conflict or controversy.

Clive Harber (1997) reminds us also that school textbooks are especially
important in developing countries, where they are often central to the teaching and learning process. The socio-political values that they represent are
often highly explicit. Omissions from the textbook can be just as interesting
as the kinds of emphasis that it observes, while the kind of language used
and the role of pictures and captions are also significant (Harber 1997,
pp. 121–2). In Kenya, for example, according to Harber, school textbooks
have tended to promote male and female stereotypes and a sexual division
of labour, with women occupying domestic and low-status positions
(Harber 1997, pp. 122–3).

It is important not to exaggerate or assume too much about the power of
textbooks to influence pupils and populations. Apple and Christian-Smith,
for all their concern about the political reverberations of textbooks, are
surely correct to add a caveat:

> We cannot assume that what is 'in' the text is actually taught. Nor can
> we assume that what is taught is actually learned. Teachers have a
> long history of mediating and transforming text material when they
> employ it in classrooms. Students bring their own classed, raced, gen-
> dered, and sexual biographies with them as well. They, too, selectively
> accept, reinterpret, and reject what counts as legitimate knowledge.
>
> (1991, p. 14)

This suggests the need for researchers to understand the nature of the reception or reading of such texts, no less than the ideology and politics that
shape them. At the same time, it can be mistaken to read off contemporary
social debates into the classroom, or vice versa; the connections must be
traced carefully in both directions rather than being taken for granted.

Reports and proceedings

Published reports are a further key source of research evidence. They are
produced most often by governments but also by organisations and pressure groups to examine a defined problem and to propose solutions. They
are useful in terms of the information that they provide on a given topic.

Thus, for example, the Spens report on secondary education, published in Britain in 1938, gives a detailed account of current provision of secondary and junior technical education, including trends in pupil numbers, free places, the length of school life, the curriculum, occupations taken up by former pupils, and teachers (Board of Education 1938, chapter 2). Similarly, a report entitled *The Future of Higher Education*, produced by the British government in 2003, gives a large amount of important and useful information on such matters as higher education funding, access to higher education and the relationship between higher education and business (Department for Education and Skills 2003).

It cannot be assumed that the information provided in such reports is always accurate, and it should be checked against other sources. The way in which such information is selected should also be carefully assessed, for it is usually designed to support a particular argument, or the government's general credibility. The report just cited, for instance, points out that:

> The Government has committed substantial investment to education. Between 1997 and 2006, the proportion of GDP spent on education will rise from 4.5 per cent to 5.6 per cent. Spending on higher education will rise from a total around £7.5 billion in 2002–03 to almost £10 billion in 2005–06 – a real terms increase of over 6 per cent each year.
>
> (DfES 2003, p. 19)

This estimate is no doubt true, but might well be only one way of reporting the figures, and it should not be ignored that in this case it gives the government an opportunity to praise its own record in higher education funding: 'This allocation is the most generous for a decade. It will stabilise the funding of universities, and allow them to make sustained progress in improving research volumes and quality and in tackling the huge backlogs in research and teaching infrastructure' (DfES 2003, p. 19). In other words, the researcher should be alert to the possibility that such information is being used selectively, and perhaps misleadingly, for political purposes.

At a deeper level, policy reports are important also as a way of revealing the kinds of assumptions that underlie policy reform. In this latter sense they provide a convenient means of understanding the official rhetoric or discourse that legitimises particular kinds of change, constructing certain possibilities but also excluding or displacing other combinations (Ball 1990, p. 18). Scott (2000) emphasises the importance of discourse in the reading of policy texts:

> The reader is not just presented with an argument and then asked to make up their mind about its merits and demerits, but positioned within a discourse – a way of understanding relations within the world – which, if it is successful, restricts and constrains the reader from

understanding the world in any other way. This discourse is characterised as common sense, whereas in fact it is merely one way of viewing
the world and is therefore ideological.

(p. 27)

They also embody the contradictions and tensions that are inherent in state
policy (Codd 1988).

The Picot report, *Administering for Excellence*, published in New Zealand
in 1988, is an interesting example of these tendencies. It made trenchant
criticisms of the failings of the education system, which it described as
'a creaky, cumbersome affair'. It saw the system as too centralised, its
administration as too complex and divided, and argued that a lack of information and choice, ineffective management practices, a widespread sense of
'powerlessness' and 'consumer dissatisfaction and disaffection' had resulted
from these basic problems. The report concluded:

Tinkering with the system will not be sufficient to achieve the improvements now required. In our view the time has come for quite radical
change, particularly to reduce the number of decision points between
the central provision of policy, funding, and services and the education
delivered by the school or institution.

(Taskforce to Review Education Administration, 1988, p. 36)

It argued therefore that administrative changes were necessary to promote
the freedom of every individual educational institution. This prescription
for reform was very limited as it did not address issues relating to the curriculum or the role of teachers, and it was rather contradictory in its embrace
of both 'choice' and 'community' (see also McCulloch 1988; Peters and
Marshall 1988).

Although individual reports can be highly revealing in their own right,
it is important to compare them with other policy reports. This may be
done by tracing the character of reports in a particular area over time. For
example, one way of interpreting the report *Educational Reconstruction*,
published in Britain in 1943 (Board of Education 1943a), is by understanding it in its longer-term context. It may be compared with educational
reports produced twenty or thirty years before, and also with those of the
1980, 1990s and early twenty-first century, such as *Choice and Diversity*
(Department for Education 1992) or *Excellence in Schools* (Department
for Education and Employment 1997). The emphasis of *Educational Reconstruction* upon the idea of secondary education for all, or of parity of esteem
between different types of school, can be traced to discern both the origins
of such notions and their later development. By the same token, it is also
useful to relate such a report to other policy representations of the same
period. In this case, links would be drawn with policy reports in education

such as the Norwood report on curriculum and examinations in secondary schools (Board of Education 1943b) and the Fleming report on public schools (Board of Education 1944), as well as the legislation to which these led, the Education Act of 1944. They may also be related to proposals in other areas being developed at the same time, such as the Beveridge report on social insurance (Beveridge 1942), as well as others of the same period. Another approach, not incompatible with these, is to develop a range of international comparisons, for example between the British Norwood report of 1943 and the Thomas report on the post-primary curriculum, published in New Zealand in 1944 (New Zealand Department of Education 1944; see also McCulloch 1994 for further details of these examples).

Similarly, in the New Zealand context, the Picot report of 1988 can be compared and contrasted with earlier policy interventions such as the Currie report of 1962 (New Zealand Department of Education 1962). The Currie report had emphasised a goal of equality of opportunity for all, and was confident that this was slowly being achieved through the beneficent auspices of State activity. By and large it tried to allay doubts and criticisms of the system, while allowing the need for further development in particular areas. It portrayed public education as non-political in character, but was itself a key instrument in transmitting an ideology that sought to satisfy clients, sponsors and the population as a whole about the value of public education. In concentrating on the gradual progress and high ideals incarnated in the education system, it either failed to face up to issues that did not fit in with this perspective, or effectively marginalised them. The impact of schooling on different social and ethnic groups, the significance of differing views on the role of education, and the social implications of administrative devices such as secondary school zoning were contained as potential sources of dissension and conflict (McCulloch 1988, p. 4). Over the following quarter-century, criticisms of the system grew from both the radical left and the right wing, leading the Picot report to try to accommodate criticisms in a new way. On this reading, to understand the aims of the Picot report of 1988 it is important to relate it not only to its immediate context but also to the development of social and political arguments over education during the preceding thirty years. In addition, this report may be interpreted not simply in relation to internal debates within New Zealand but to the rise of a so-called 'New Right' movement internationally, for example in the United States and Britain (see also McCulloch 1988, pp. 10–11; Openshaw 1995).

As sources of evidence, some reports offer more than others for researchers. There are those that have been developed over a number of years, following extensive consultation with large numbers of groups and individuals. These often run to several volumes, including appendices of oral and written evidence provided by witnesses. This was very common in the nineteenth century, but even in the past fifty years such an approach has been adopted, for example in the Robbins report on British higher education (Ministry of Education 1963b) and the Dearing review of qualifications for sixteen- to nineteen-year-olds (Dearing 1996). These are valuable quarries of data for researchers, still bearing in mind the caution that has already been emphasised for the use of such sources. On the other hand, there has been a trend in recent decades towards the publication of reports that are short and photogenic to promote their public appeal. This type is in some ways less useful for researchers, although such reports do reflect contemporary fashions, and they are especially treacherous as a source of evidence.

A further issue about using reports as documentary sources is that they should not be assumed to represent everyday reality in a straightforward way. Social practices should not be read off from policy proposals. The influence of reports is often far less than their authors imagine, and they may be read and interpreted in ways that are not anticipated. Thus, although the Plowden report of 1967 (Department of Education and Science 1967) supported a progressive, child-centred approach to primary education, this does not mean that primary schools uniformly adopted such an approach. Those responsible for implementing new policies, such as schools and teachers in the case of education, may find a number of ways of accommodating, subverting or openly resisting them (see for example Bowe and Ball 1992; Helsby and McCulloch 1997). This often leads to significant differences between the assumptions embodied in reports, on the one hand, and organisational practices, on the other.

Another kind of official publication is the proceedings of parliamentary debates and committees. In Britain these are known as Hansard, after Thomas Hansard, who began publishing the debates of the House of Commons and the House of Lords in 1812. This became an official government publication from 1909, and, as Tosh observes, 'Few other sources convey so well the public face of political discourse' (2002, p. 63). It is now available online. The transcripts of daily debates, written ministerial statements and written answers to questions may be found at http://www. parliament.the-stationery-office.co.uk. Legislation, unpublished government information and official publications are accessible at http://www.hmso. gov.uk. Bills currently being considered by Parliament, the proceedings of committees, parliamentary publications and the register of interests of Members of Parliament are at http://www.parliament.uk. This latter source includes full proceedings, oral evidence and reports of select committees established in different areas, such as the Education and Skills Select Committee.

In the United States, the Congressional Record provides a similar service, also accessible on the Internet (http://www.gpoaccess.gov/crecord/index.html). First published in 1873, this provides up-to-date and complete proceedings of debates in the House of Representatives and the Senate,

Congressional bills, the history of bills and the House Journal. For example, it includes a record of a debate held in the House of Representatives on 14 May 2003 to commemorate the forty-ninth anniversary of the Supreme Court's landmark decision on *Brown* v. *Board of Education*, intended to eliminate racial segregation in the public education system. Part of this debate is a speech by James E. Clyburn of South Carolina, a former chairman of the Congressional Black Caucus, reprinted here as Case Study 4.

Case Study 4

Congressional Record, United States of America
Debate in House of Representatives commemorating the forty-ninth anniversary of *Brown* v. *Board of Education*, 14 May 2003
Speech by Mr Clyburn, South Carolina

Mr Speaker, I come to the floor tonight because I am a little bit concerned about where we are and how we got here. Over the next year, in fact, if I may, next May 17, we will celebrate the 50th anniversary of Brown v. Board of Education of Topeka, Kansas. That means that come Saturday we will celebrate the 49th anniversary. Over the next year we will hear a lot about Brown, and, in fact, on May 17, 50 years to the day of that decision, there will be a new park opened in Topeka, Kansas, to honor the case.

I do not begrudge the people of Topeka, Kansas, for their new park, but I do have a real problem as a former history teacher with revisionism because Brown took on the name for some very unusual reasons. If we were to go by tradition and name cases based upon the alphabet, this case would have been called Belton, because the case coming out of Delaware, one of the five that led to Brown, was Belton against Gebhart. If the case had taken on the name of the first to file, it would have been called Briggs because Briggs v. Elliot, which started in South Carolina, was first filed on May 16, 1950. Nine months later, the Brown case was filed, February 28, 1951, and 3 months later, May 23, the Davis case in Virginia was filed, and somewhere between January and April of 1951, Bolling against Sharpe, the D.C. case, was filed.

Mr Speaker, I point this out tonight because the people of Clarendon County, South Carolina, that I am proud to represent here in this body, the birthplace of our current Chair's parents, both his mother and father were born in Clarendon County School District No. 1, where this case originated.

continued on facing page

So tonight I wanted to come to the floor to put on the record the exact history of Brown because so much is being said about this case, and very little of it is accurate.

In a 1947 meeting on the campus of Allen University in Columbia, South Carolina, Reverend J.A. DeLaine heard a speech challenging the ministers who were independent from the system to get involved in helping to right some of the wrongs that existed in our society. Reverend DeLaine left that campus that day and went back home to Summerton, South Carolina, where he began to meet with his church members, and in 1947, he asked the parents to petition the superintendent of schools to ask for a school bus.

At that time parents were sending their kids to school having to walk 9 or 10 miles one way. They were denied a school bus, and so they pooled their resources and raised money to buy a used bus to transport their kids to school. Gas was expensive, and the bus was old, and it kept breaking down. So they went to a local farmer, Levi Pearson, and in 1948, Levi Pearson filed a lawsuit asking for his children, who at that time were walking 9 miles one way to school, to be provided transportation.

We have got to understand that all the white kids in that county were riding school buses, but black kids were denied a school bus.

The case was thrown out because Levi Pearson's farm was in both school districts, both the Manning school district and the Summerton school district, and on a technicality they decided that Levi Pearson's house was in the Manning school district and not the Summerton school district. So the case was thrown out.

In 1949, Reverend DeLaine met with the NAACP [National Association for the Advancement of Colored People] and petitioned the all-white county school board to provide equality of education for their children. It, of course, was denied. So in October of that year, they all met in the home of Harry Briggs and his wife Eliza.

Anybody who comes into my office today will see on my wall a great picture of Eliza Briggs. For as long as I serve in this august body, Mrs. Briggs' picture will have a prominent place on the wall of my office.

Mr. Harry Briggs was an attendant at a filling station. He was fired from his job for signing the petition. They eventually moved to Florida where they lived out their productive lives, moving back to Clarendon when they were no longer able to be productive.

continued on next page

In 1950, the school board refused to respond to the petition, and then in February 1951, the State of South Carolina entered the case on behalf of the school board. So not only were these people denied by their county school board, but now they were being fought by their entire State mechanism.

In 1951, the State of South Carolina decided that it would use all of its resources to preserve a separate but equal, inherently unequal, school district.

In 1953, the Supreme Court heard arguments, and on May 17, 1954, 4 years and 1 day from the time the case was first filed in Summerton, South Carolina, these people got what they sought, and that was a decision by the United States Supreme Court that separate but equal was inherently unequal.

I want to share with the folks who are looking in tonight a couple of statements from three descendants of these, I would call, brave, heroic people. They are all here in Washington today, and on yesterday here in Washington, here is what Harold Gibson had to say. He said that 'my mother and father was faced with a choice. Take your name off of the petition or be evicted from your home. They were evicted on Christmas Eve.'

Ms. Annie Gibson, Harold Gibson's mother, her picture is on the wall of my office, and it, too, will always be there for as long as I am here.

Listen to what the DeLaine brothers had to say about their dad, J.A. DeLaine, whose father spearheaded the case: Our house was burned to the ground. Shots were fired into the new home into which we had moved. When my father fired back, local authorities issued a warrant for his arrest. For their safety, the family fled in 1955 to Buffalo, New York, and it was not until the year 2000, 25 years later, that the State of South Carolina dropped the charges against Reverend DeLaine. Now, it was 45 years later from the time of the charges, but 25 years after his death.

I bring this out tonight because when I went to work for John West in 1971, John West, the Governor of South Carolina, received a letter from Reverend DeLaine. Reverend DeLaine wrote Governor West and said that he was getting up in years, his health was beginning to fail, and he wanted to come home to South Carolina to die. John West asked me to look into the case and to plan a homecoming for Reverend DeLaine. He wanted us to have a ceremony that would mark an end to this episode and to be a new beginning for the State of South Carolina.

continued on facing page

We could not bring Reverend DeLaine back home because there living in Clarendon County was one of the original people who swore out the warrant, and in spite of the Governor's pleadings, the law enforcement officers' pleadings, he refused to drop the case.

So Reverend DeLaine came back as far as Charlotte, North Carolina, where he eventually died and is buried.

Now, the case of Briggs. Listen to what Nathaniel Briggs, says: 'My father worked at a gas station. It was owned by the mayor of Summerton. He lost his job and my mother lost her job at the local hotel.'

Mr. Speaker, I want to close my comments by thanking our Chair of the Congressional Black Caucus for organizing this Special Order tonight, and to close on this note. As historic as this is, the fact of the matter is we have not gotten there yet. In fact, come August, the State of South Carolina will be hearing a case in the same courtroom where the Brown case started as Briggs against Elliott. In that courtroom, we will be listening to arguments over whether or not it is constitutional to still underfund school districts with high populations of black students.

In South Carolina today, the law is that we in the State are required to provide a public education, but we are not required to provide an adequate education. And, therefore, schoolchildren in school districts with high black populations are not being funded to the same level as school kids in other districts. And I want to point out, as I close, the inequity. Today, in South Carolina, school districts with higher percentages of African American students have 313 fewer State and local dollars, fewer than students with school districts of low levels of African Americans. This inequity translates into a gap of $8,000 a year per classroom and more than $1 million a year per school. That tells the story.

So though Brown is now 49 years old, equal educational opportunities have not come to Clarendon County or South Carolina yet. Hopefully, this case that will be heard in August will be decided before May 17, 2004, and decided by law and equity, so that, hopefully, as we celebrate the 50th anniversary of Brown, we can celebrate the beginning of equitable education for black people in Clarendon County, South Carolina, and our Nation. I thank the Chairman for allowing me this time.

Clyburn's speech, with its many rich stories, is a fascinating example of documentary testimony, once again freely available on the Internet, and a matter of public record. It would be difficult to test the accuracy of some of the claims made in it, although the background of the speaker and the context of the speech command respect. It provides an important perspective on the issues raised by *Brown* v. *Board of Education*, and one that makes clear connections between education and inequality, poverty, ethnicity, economics, housing, religion and the law. Moreover, Clyburn's account illuminates a close relationship between the past and the present, as he recalls events that took place half a century before and relates them to issues that have continued to be problematic. Lastly, it gives eloquent testimony to the interconnections between the public and the private arenas. It makes use of a public platform to raise awareness about a key set of concerns with local and national implications. In order to do so, it brings out the ways in which individual lives and families have been affected by these broader debates.

A further type of publicly available documentary source material of a quasi-official kind consists of datasets produced by governments, organisations and research teams. These make possible what is usually referred to as secondary analysis, defined by Catherine Hakim as 'any further analysis of an existing dataset which presents interpretation, conclusions, or knowledge additional to, or different from, those presented in the first report on the inquiry as a whole and its main results' (Hakim 1982, p. 1). This would include the development of more focused or detailed reports based on such data, and analyses framed in different theories or techniques. There is a wide range of sources of secondary data available in education and the social sciences more generally that have been archived and are available online. These may be used either singly or in combination, and also as a complementary strategy alongside other research. The existence of large national datasets of this type also makes it possible to develop cross-national and comparative research (see also for example Burton 2000b; Gorard 2001, 2002).

Population census reports, for example, can be employed for both social and historical research. Hakim reminds us that researchers should be able to make use of census material of three different types: original census records (when these become publicly available), statistical results published in census reports and the commentaries on the results of each census conducted (Hakim 1980, p. 552). She points out, too, that census commentaries reflect the historical character of the census, and the issues and concerns that have been current during its development since its beginnings (in 1841 in Britain, 1880 in the United States):

> If the census is a snapshot of the nation at a particular point in time, the
> commentaries reveal how and why the camera was angled, how and

why the picture was framed in a certain way . . . Census commentaries reveal the subjectivity, historical relativity, and cultural relativity that often lie behind the statistical facts presented in the published census reports.

(Hakim 1980, p. 553)

British census material is available online at http://census.ac.uk. The most recent census of the population in the United Kingdom, conducted on 29 April 2001, forms the basis for an extensive database and a number of printed reports and datasets.

Other British public datasets in education and the social sciences that may be accessed fully or partly online include *Social Trends* (http://www. statistics.gov.uk), an annual production which draws together social and economic data from many different government departments and other organisations to develop a broad picture of British society as a whole. There are thirteen chapters focusing on different social policy areas – population, households and families, education, labour market, income and wealth, expenditure, health, social protection, crime and justice, housing, environment, transport, lifestyles and social participation. The UK Data Archive (http://www.data-archive.ac.uk) is a depository for digital data in the social sciences and humanities, and aims to support the secondary use of quantitative and qualitative data. It also houses two specialist units, the History Data Service and Qualidata – Qualitative Data Service – and gives access to international data through co-operative agreements and memberships with archives around the world. In June 2003 a web-based International Data Service (IDS) was launched as part of the Economic and Social Data Service, sponsored by the ESRC and JISC, to provide support for a number of international datasets of macro-economic time series (see http://www.mimas.ac.uk/macro_econ/).

Two major datasets related to education are those of the National Child Development Study (NCDS) (http://www.data-archive.ac.uk) and the Youth Cohort Study of England and Wales (YCS) (http://www.dfes. gov.uk/statistics). The NCDS is a longitudinal study tracking the lives of those living in Great Britain who were born between 3 and 9 March 1958. It has involved six stages so far to monitor the physical, educational and social development of this birth cohort, with survey sweeps in 1965 (age 7), 1969 (age 11), 1974 (age 16), 1981 (age 23), 1985 (age 33) and 1999–2000 (age 41–2). The YCS is also a longitudinal programme that monitors the behaviour and decisions of representative samples of young people aged sixteen and over in transition from compulsory education to further or higher education and the labour market. This has covered ten cohorts, the first in 1985 and the most recent in 2001, and a large number of surveys based on these. Surveys examine young people's education and labour market experience, training and qualifications and a range of other issues.

Newspapers and periodicals

Tosh suggests that the press constitutes the most important type of public source material. In particular, he notes, it records the political and social views that are most influential at any particular time (and place, it might be added); it provides a day-to-day record of events; and it sometimes offers thorough enquiries into specific issues deemed to be of public concern (Tosh 2002, pp. 63–4). Newspapers, first recorded in Germany in 1609, became a public institution first in the Dutch Republic, especially in Amsterdam, in the seventeenth century. By the eighteenth century daily newspapers were an important part of social life in England also, where about fifteen million newspapers were sold in the year 1792 (Briggs and Burke 2002, p. 70). Magazines and periodicals also developed from this time, for example *The Tatler* from 1709 and *The Spectator* from 1711. With the fall of newspaper tax in 1836 from fourpence to one penny, press circulation increased and many new dailies, weeklies, monthlies and quarterlies were produced, a development encouraged further during the nineteenth century with the growth of a literate mass reading public (Secord 2000, p. 33).

One interesting and helpful example of using newspapers as a documentary source is that of Peter Cunningham, who has examined the development of the image of the teacher in the British press over the forty years from 1950 to 1990 (Cunningham 1992). He does so by comparing newspaper coverage of teachers in 1950, 1970 and 1990, using *The Times* as the unofficial 'newspaper of record' during this period in Britain and the major mass circulation newspapers of the political right and left. Over this period, Cunningham is able to trace a number of continuities in how teachers are represented in the press, notably in relation to issues about the nature of their professionalism and professional status. These newspapers also reflect growing political criticisms of teachers over this time, and the establishment of a demonology of teachers and teaching. This latter trend and its encouragement by the popular press has also been noted by Ball, who described this as a 'discourse of derision' that had major political and social implications (Ball 1990). Warburton and Saunders (1996) develop this further through an examination of political cartoons featuring the professional culture of teachers that have appeared in British newspapers since the 1970s, to buttress and extend the messages of the reports and leading articles.

The treatment of social and political issues in the popular press is exemplified in the British *Daily Mirror* and its coverage of Lady Morgan, director of government relations at 10 Downing Street and a key adviser to the Prime Minister, Tony Blair, on her decision to send her son to a private school rather than a state school. The newspaper's leading article (on 1 October 2002, carried online at http://www.mirror.co.uk/news) was headed 'LABOUR PEER'S A CLASS APART', and appears as Case Study 5.

Case Study 5

The Daily Mirror, UK, 1 October 2002
Leading article – 'Labour peer's a class apart'

A key aide of Tony Blair is sending her son to a £9,000-a-year private college instead of one of eight comprehensives near her home.

The decision by Sally Morgan, 43, one of the most powerful figures at No 10, angered delegates at the Labour conference in Blackpool yesterday.

A Downing Street insider said: 'It sends out all the wrong messages.'

Transport Union boss Bob Crow said: 'These people should practise what they preach.'

Baroness Morgan was helping Tony Blair draft his speech to the Labour conference yesterday – while her son set out on his 40-minute journey to a private school.

Baroness Morgan, 43, chose the £9,000-a-year independent boys' school over eight mixed or boys' comprehensives within a few miles of her £1 million home.

The revelation angered delegates at the Blackpool conference where Ministers have repeatedly praised the State system.

But Lady Morgan said in a statement issued to the Daily Mirror last night: 'I tried and failed to get my child into two good local comprehensive schools. In the end, as a parent, I have to put him first.'

The Premier is today due to stress his personal commitment to the comprehensive ideal with a vow to give every child the opportunities enjoyed by the privileged few.

Union boss Bob Crow, of the RMT, said: 'These people should practise what they preach. If State schools are so good and they have to put so much investment in them, why don't they lead by example and send their children there?'

Labour MP Harry Barnes said: 'We should not be making it easier for schools in the private sector.'

A Downing Street insider added: 'They've been terrified this news would leak out. When the Government is stressing the importance of public services, somebody at the very centre looks to be showing she has no faith in them.'

Lady Morgan, who earns £120,000 a year as director of Government relations at No 10, is among a handful of advisers at the very heart of New Labour and a close friend of Tony and Cherie Blair. Her 12-year-old son, who previously attended a state primary school with his

continued on next page

younger brother, goes to his new school by train and Tube from Wandsworth in South London.

Lady Morgan and her husband, successful barrister John Lyons, are paying £8,307 a year for his schooling – plus £423 for lunches.

The London college has an impressive exam record and excellent music, sports and drama facilities.

In contrast, Chestnut Grove comprehensive, a five-minute walk from the family home, is known by locals as a 'sink' school. But there are other schools close by with far higher standards and better results.

Lady Morgan told Mr Blair about her decision immediately. He is believed to have taken the view that it was a private matter for parents.

This *Daily Mirror* article is useful as a source in that it provides evidence (which would clearly require checking) about attitudes to state schools and private schools in contemporary Britain. It is a highly partisan report, which itself is significant as an indicator of the biases of the tabloid media, though not necessarily of the general public. It relates the public to the private in a broader sense too. It deliberately personalises a controversial public issue in its critical commentary of an individual who is not an elected politician, and who is a public figure only in a rather tangential sense. It also gives details about her husband, who is even less of a public figure, and of her children. Overall, the article is a striking illustration of the overlapping and intermeshing nature of the public and private domains in contemporary society.

An example of a broadsheet newspaper with a smaller readership than the *Daily Mirror* but with some standing among the left-liberal middle class in Britain is *The Guardian*. As a documentary source this newspaper should also be scanned warily for bias and inaccuracy. It is, however, a significant and convenient resource, especially for its online facility, which includes a searchable archive on any topic carried in the newspaper since 1998 (http://www.guardian.co.uk/). It also has extensive sections on arts, books, business, education, society, sport, travel, and UK and world news and other topics. In its education section, for example, it gives detailed news features on schools, higher education, further education and students, with a further category of general comment and analysis (http://www. education.guardian.co.uk/). The further education section for 21 June 2003 includes the full transcript of a speech by the school standards minister, David Miliband, presented to a conference of the Association of Colleges in Cambridge on 18 June. This speech, entitled 'Vocational education: quality and status', calls for an end to the 'pernicious snobbery' that has afflicted vocational training in Britain, an intriguing blend of historical perspective and policy argument.

Newspapers may also be useful for the basic information that they can provide for historians and social researchers. In New Zealand, for instance, on 30 May 1989 the daily evening newspaper the *Auckland Star* printed a chart of 'pupil migration' between secondary schools over the previous five years, based on figures compiled by the Department of Education. This chart showed that some schools, such as Auckland Grammar School and Epsom Girls' Grammar School, had gained several hundred pupils from the enrolment zones of other schools over the previous five years. On the other hand, some other schools, such as Seddon High School, Green Bay, Nga Tapuwae, Tamaki College and Henderson High School, had lost several hundred pupils from their own zone to other schools over the same period. At the top of the scale, Auckland Grammar had 228 potential third-formers in its zone in 1989, but had 345 third-form enrolments (151 per cent of potential in-zone recruits), while Henderson High, at the bottom of the table, had 376 potential third-formers in its zone but only 144 third-form enrolments (38 per cent). Over a five-year period, Auckland Grammar had gained a total of 771 pupils from outside its own zone at the expense of other schools; Henderson High had lost 811 pupils to other schools from within its own zone during the same period (*Auckland Star* 1989).

It was fascinating also that there was a close correlation between this situation and the enrolment scheme introduced for the 1991 pupil intake. It was a simple matter for me to note which schools were to have home zones under the new arrangements that were introduced in 1991, alongside the table published in the *Auckland Star*. This revealed that the top fifteen schools in the table, all of which had attracted large numbers of out-of-zone pupils over the past five years, would have home zones under the new scheme. On the other hand, the bottom thirteen schools in the table, all of which had lost many pupils in their own areas to other schools even when no zoning was in operation, were now to have no home zone at all, and would have no protection to maintain a level of pupil enrolments. The implication of this was that the free market would operate for the least popular schools but not for the most popular schools, whose local parents would retain their rights to enrol their children at them (McCulloch 1991a, p. 161; the five-year chart published in the *Auckland Star* is reprinted in McCulloch 1991a, p. 162).

Different parts of the newspapers may also provide interesting and relevant material for researchers. For example, the advertising section might give clues to differential house pricing dependent on location in the 'Grammar Zone'. The letters columns may well give expression to the frustrations and protests of parents, while leading articles often provide a platform for a range of viewpoints on current issues. Newspapers may also be used well in combination with other documentary sources. As we have already seen (Chapter 4 above, see Case Study 3), where they are accessible to researchers, archival sources may well be very helpful and indeed give key insights not only into the policy but also into the individual human experiences involved, which may be set alongside the newspaper coverage. Magazines may also be of use. General periodicals with more considered and lengthy pieces of journalism may provide instructive examples of problems and the responses to them. In this case, for instance, the monthly periodical *Auckland Metro* has been a continuing source of contemporary comment on related issues, from pieces on the mystique of schools such as Auckland Grammar School ('The Auckland Grammar mystique', *Auckland Metro* 1984) to investigations into the gentrification of suburbs and the effects of this on their schools ('Three months in another town', *Auckland Metro* 1986).

Specialist magazines are a further useful public media source of commentary and information. In Britain, for example, political weekly periodicals include the conservative-leaning *Spectator* (see also www.spectator.co.uk) and the left-wing radical *New Statesman* (www.newstatesman.co.uk). The *Economist* is another well established weekly periodical that focuses on economic and financial trends (www.economist.co.uk). In the area of education, the *Times Educational Supplement*, for schools and further education (www.tes.co.uk), and the *Times Higher Education Supplement* (www.thes. co.uk), for universities, also supply detailed source material. In all such instances the researcher may use a short run of magazines intensively to focus on a specific context or incident, or inspect them over a longer period to gauge continuities and changes over time.

Some periodicals and magazines are specialist in the sense that they have a limited circulation within a specific organisation or network. School magazines are an example of this kind of source, produced for internal consumption and for an audience of parents, alumni and others associated with the school. Such sources provide a significant record of the institution, on behalf of the institution itself, designed to celebrate the successes and where possible to avoid mention of difficulties and failures. As J.A. Mangan notes of the school magazines of the English public schools of the late nineteenth century, they have a self-appointed role as an official record of school life, and therefore perpetuate established values rather than challenge them (Mangan 1981/1986, p. 243). They constitute overall a key source on the 'beliefs, attitudes and values of an era', which in the case of the English public schools reflect in many cases an emphasis given to games and sports as opposed to academic pursuits (Mangan 1981/1986, p. 245). At the same time, unofficial magazines, or items included deliberately or not that question the dominant orthodoxy, are important clues to the debates and conflicts that may well exist beneath the placid surface.

Fiction

Creative and imaginative literature, or fiction, is a further potential source of documentary evidence for social researchers and historians. Again, historians are prone to be dismissive or at best grudging in their acknowledgement of the worth of such material. Marwick, for instance, insists that for the 'concrete facts' of everyday existence, wage rates, living standards and environmental conditions, the historian will prefer if possible 'not to take the word of a novelist, but will turn to government papers, statistical series, company records, trade union archives, private correspondence, houses still in existence from the era he [*sic*] is studying, or their remains' (Marwick 1981, p. 147). Once the historian has established the record from such sources, according to Marwick, a vivid example might be drawn from a novel or poem to illustrate the point, but not to prove it. Although it might be 'fun' and 'fashionable' to work with novels, films or paintings, Marwick avers that 'this is not evidence of some superior virtue, or sensibility; in fact, most of what we know about most periods in the past will continue to come from the more conventional sources' (Marwick 2001, p. 188).

None the less, fiction can be a telling source of evidence if carefully used. Novels, for instance, have significant potential for social researchers and historians alike. Novels developed in their modern form in the first half of the eighteenth century in the work of such pioneers as Defoe, Richardson and Fielding, and the term itself was not established in its modern form until the end of that century (Watt 1957). Watt points out the importance of the novel as a device for expressing individual experience. John Bunyan's *Pilgrim's Progress* may be taken as a prime example of the religious form of such experience, with Daniel Defoe's *Robinson Crusoe* the archetypal economic individualist. According to Watt, indeed, so far as the development of modern society is concerned, 'The novel is the form of literature which most fully reflects [its] individualist and innovating reorientation' (1957, p. 13). This feature of the novel gives it particular scope to provide not only vivid social commentary but also insights into the private dilemmas of modern life.

Some historians are willing to endorse this potential, even if Marwick is loath to do so. For example, Steven Connor is emphatic that 'The novel has always been a useful resource for history and historians' (Connor 1996, p. 1). It is the freedom that the novel allows to explore individualism and individuality that especially captures Connor's enthusiasm, as he continues: 'Typically, the novel promises a view of that fine grain of events and experiences which otherwise tend to shrink to invisibility in the long perspectives of historical explanation. Novels seem to have some of the authority of the eye-witness account, in providing the historian with enactment, particularity and individual testimony' (Connor 1996, p. 1). Moreover,

Connor adds, 'Novels also represent a meeting point between the individual and the general, bridging the isolated subjectivity and the peopled world, and giving an individual dimension to the otherwise abstract or disembodied nature of shared norms and values' (Connor 1996, p. 1). They therefore mediate between the domestic and the economic, the private and the public. Pamela Fox also develops this point to investigate the public/private dynamic of British working-class culture through a study of the development of working-class novels in Britain from 1890 to 1945 (Fox 1994).

A number of social researchers have identified similar issues in the use of the novel as a documentary source. Morroe Berger argues that 'there is no intrinsic reason that the novel should not seek to instruct or to illumine social institutions' (Berger 1977, p. 5), and indeed suggests that there has been a convergence between the novel and social science, or between the real and imagined worlds. Novels can deal with social institutions either directly, through events or characters that can be used to explore broad themes, or through narrative intrusions that may not carry the story forward but offer commentary on contemporary society. Even more resolutely, Joan Rockwell develops a strong case for the use of literature in the systematic study of society (Rockwell 1974). She declares that literature is neither private fantasy nor simply entertainment, but is indeed a product of society, as much so as any institution such as the family or the State (Rockwell 1974, pp. 3, vii). It is descriptive in that it provides information on such aspects as the state of technology, laws, customs, social structure and institutions, and it also points to values and attitudes especially at times of fundamental social changes (Rockwell 1974, p. 4). Therefore, she insists, the 'patterned connection between society and fiction is so discernable and so reliable that literature ought to be added to the regular tools of social investigation' (Rockwell 1974, p. 3).

In the area of education, for example, there are large numbers of works of fiction that may be analysed as documentary sources, albeit with caution. Children were rarely to be seen in English literature until towards the end of the eighteenth century, but have been making up for this ever since. According to Philip Collins (1963), Charles Dickens was the first English novelist in whose stories children are frequent and central, rather than minor characters in the background (p. 1). Dickens's novels, moreover, were informed by his broad experience of visiting and working for a range of educational institutions. Such works as *Oliver Twist, Nicholas Nickleby, David Copperfield* and *Great Expectations* powerfully evoke the experiences of childhood, in such a manner that, as Collins suggests, 'no one but a creative writer could do: a writer, moreover, equipped with a very special kind of memory and insight as well as with unfailing felicity of expression' (Collins 1963, p. 208). Thomas Hughes's *Tom Brown's Schooldays* (1857) similarly evoked the culture of the reformed, Arnoldian English public schools of the nineteenth century. According to Jeffrey Richards (1988), the public school story of the kind created by *Tom Brown's Schooldays* provides significant evidence first of all of a factual kind in relation for example to customs, practices, conditions and methods, secondly about the experience of pupils, thirdly about the promotion of particular ideas, attitudes and educational and social policies, and lastly, through the development of a distinct genre, about the cumulative cultural image of the public schools (see also Cadogan and Craig 1986).

One potential problem in the use of such literature is that it tends to dwell on standard types and settings, to the extent that less familiar institutions are ignored. For example, Ian Carter's study of university fiction in Britain since the Second World War (1990) was based on 196 works of fiction based in universities published since 1945, of which most were on Oxford and Cambridge, especially Oxford. As Carter notes,

> Despite their apparent diversity, almost all British university novels play modest variations on one of three linked stories: how an undergraduate at Oxford (usually) or Cambridge came to wisdom; how a don at Oxford (usually) or Cambridge was stabbed in the back physically or professionally, sometimes surviving to rule the college; and how rotten life was as a student or teacher outside Oxford and Cambridge.
>
> (Carter 1990, p. 15)

They can therefore be distorted and stereotyped representations of social life.

Novels about schools, likewise, are dominated in Britain at least by images of the elite public school, although there are many contributions nevertheless that provide insight into other types of schooling. Edward Blishen's novel *Roaring Boys: A Schoolmaster's Agony*, published in 1955, is one such, based on an urban secondary modern school, 'Stonehill Street', that bore a close resemblance to schools in which he himself had taught. According to Blishen himself, 'If my story is not literally true, I have tried to make it true in a wider sense' (Blishen 1955, p. 1). It stands out from a proliferation of fiction set in schools through its understanding of daily life. The institution itself is observed in detail, but, as Spolton remarks, 'it comes alive from its descriptions of the boys' (1962–3, p. 129). The school is depicted vividly as in this passage early in the novel:

> It began in the morning as I walked into the district. I always tried to look invisible, but it didn't work. A group of Class 2 boys would catch sight of me. 'Hiya,' they would call, and giggle maliciously. I would turn purple and nod and try to hurry past. They would tail me. 'I say, old boys,' they would say in affected accents, 'how's the world treating you?' . . . And the school would come into view, as unkind as a

prison. It wasn't of the worst period of State school architecture; it was only two storeys high, instead of three, there were warm red bricks distributed among the grey ones, and a curve here and there in the roof-line had a mollifying effect. But the architect was definitely thinking of prisons when he designed it. Its gates were so obviously meant to be locked; its high walls were so plainly meant to imprison; its hard playgrounds were so suggestive, not of play, but of penal exercise. And over the doors were worn announcements in stone: 'Senior Boys', 'Senior Girls'. These words were no longer relevant, but their terse statements of categories made it easy to imagine the mute pinafored ranks of fifty years before.

(Blishen 1955, pp. 6–7)

Blishen's novel is also a useful source of social comment about the inferior position of the secondary modern schools, for example in its observations about the plan to change the name of the school:

There was a time, I believe, when some of the old elementary schools were known by numbers. Most of the new secondary modern schools, like Stonehill Street, still staggered along under the burden of names derived from the roads in which they were to be found. An essential feature of the 1944 Education Act was that all secondary schools should appear to be of the same standing. Now, there is as little similarity of prestige between the names 'Sir Basil Montmorency Grammar School' and 'Stonehill Street Secondary Modern' as there is between the names 'Julian' and 'Bert'. A great deal of renaming, therefore, was considered necessary.

(Blishen 1955, p. 70)

Eventually it is decided to call the school 'The Sir Thomas Crackenthorpe' after a seventeenth-century nobleman, and the headmaster, Mr Penny, endeavours to explain this to the school: '"It's not," he told the school, "that we're ashamed of our old name, but we're going to have a . . . a . . .".' Hunting for an epithet, he found it in the boys' own vocabulary. "We're going to have a *posher* name," he said' (Blishen 1955, pp. 71–2).

Blishen's observations of the pupils and teachers are no less incisive. His general commentary is very much to the point:

I thought often of the well-dressed, cosy crocodiles of prep school boys I had led, not so long before, on their chattering way to the playing-fields. By contrast, a crocodile of Stonehill Street boys was a procession of scarecrows. The staff in their neat suiting, even in their old sports jackets and flannels, looked like visitors from another world. And, in fact, in Stonehill Street two worlds collided. You couldn't help seeing it that way. The masters and the boys had very different backgrounds. And even though a teacher managed in the end to master the manners of his charges, it was always an act of mastery and never an act of intimacy. Even the most experienced members of the staff would discuss the boys as barbarous Celts might have been discussed by a Roman garrison.

(Blishen 1955, p. 59)

He also provides sympathetic and compelling portraits of some individual pupils, such as 'Roy Jessup', who had been selected at the age of eleven for a grammar school education, but who came from a poor home, spoke badly and was shabbily dressed, and was sent to Stonehill Street instead, eventually to take his examinations there.

Such fictional accounts can therefore be significant sources for social researchers and historians. They are helpful for their discussions of the present and of the past, as well as of how institutions and society have developed over time. It is possible to combine them with other sources, and to compare and contrast them with a range of other published accounts. Blishen's novel, for example, may usefully be contrasted with Eric James's treatise *Education and Leadership* (1951) in order to assess something of the practical and everyday effects of educational and social thinking. They also provide useful social commentaries in their own right, and provide a means of imagining individual sensibilities and private hopes and grief.

In general, then, printed media and literature comprise a wide-ranging and potentially rich set of documentary source material for historians and social researchers that is convenient and inexpensive to use. Nor do the examples chosen in this chapter by any means exhaust the possibilities for research of this type. Imaginative use of other material from comics to cigarette cards, poetry to plays may also bring useful and interesting results. All of these sources are on the record; they need not be hidden from our view.

Suggestions for further reading

Blishen, E. (1955) *Roaring Boys: A Schoolmaster's Agony*, Thames and Hudson, London

Briggs, A., Burke, P. (2002) *A Social History of the Media: From Gutenberg to the Internet*, Polity, Cambridge

Burton, D. (2000) Secondary data analysis. In D. Burton (ed.), *Research Training for Social Scientists: A Handbook for Postgraduate Researchers*, Sage, London, pp. 347–62

McCulloch, G. (1991a) School zoning, equity and freedom: the case of New Zealand, *Journal of Education Policy*, 6/2, pp. 155–68

Marsden, W.E. (2001) *The School Textbook: Geography, History, and Social Studies*, Woburn, London

Rockwell, J. (1974) *Fact in Fiction: The Use of Literature in the Systematic Study of Society*, Routledge and Kegan Paul, London

Scott, D. (2000) *Reading Educational Research and Policy*, RoutledgeFalmer, London

http://www.gpoaccess.gov/crecord/index.html

http://www.parliament.gov.uk

6 Life and Times

Diaries, Letters and Autobiographies

The well known injunction to say it with flowers but not in ink has been widely ignored by individuals wishing to express or to explain themselves, whether to themselves or to others. Diaries, letters and autobiographies are usually categorised as personal documents, because they are produced by individuals, and they shed a great deal of light on personal and private attitudes, aspirations and ambitions. Naturally there has been some variety in the ways in which such documents have been interpreted. The psychologist Gordon Allport noted in the 1940s: 'It is in large part through the human, or personal document, that we learn what goes on in people's minds' (Allport 1947, p. viii). He argued that the everyday struggles of ordinary people had become a prime concern of social scientists, and that therefore such documents would become of increasing significance in social scientific research. At the same time, the sociologist Robert Angell emphasised the importance of personal documents for showing how social situations appeared to the actors in them, and defined them as documents that reveal 'a participant's view of experiences in which he [*sic*] has been involved' (Angell 1947, p. 177). More recently, Burgess has proposed that the key issue in common in such documents is that they all 'present an individual's subjective view of social life' (Burgess 1984a, p. 125). Plummer acknowledges the wide range of disciplinary emphases that have been applied to such documents, but insists that they have in common what he calls 'a concern to present the subjective point of view of a participant' (Plummer 2001, p. 18). Moreover, according to Plummer, 'They are all first-order accounts which attempt to enter the subjective world of informants, taking them seriously on their own terms and thereby providing first hand, intimately involved accounts of life' (Plummer 2001, p. 18).

Nevertheless, even with this type of document, it should not be assumed that their value as sources is confined to a personal or private domain. Many diaries, letters and autobiographies are highly revealing about public issues and debates, whether as commentaries on contemporary incidents or changes, or because they provide a record of meetings or other events in which the author is a witness. Indeed, they often constitute the most significant documentary sources in such cases, because they provide compelling witness accounts by the people involved, as opposed to the bland official statements commonly encountered in committee minutes.

A further issue is that diaries, letters and autobiographies vary in their nature and value as documentary sources, whether in relation to the personal or to the public. They vary, first, as categories of sources. Diaries are personal accounts with entries produced on a regular basis, usually soon after the event being described, and so are usually seen as especially reliable sources. On the other hand, they may still be biased or inaccurate, and some diaries are kept not only as a private record but with an eye to subsequent circulation or publication. Letters are produced as sources of information between one individual and another, or sometimes for a group of people. Although they also comprise significant evidence, the nature of the relationship involved between the sender and the recipient needs to be scrutinised with care. Autobiographies are often important as recollections of the individual's life, the struggles in which they have been involved and the changes they have witnessed, but are often produced many years after the events being recounted and in many cases for the purposes of self-justification. Frequently, diaries, letters and autobiographies are useful as complementary sources. It can be enlightening to compare (and contrast) an individual's contemporary account as recorded in their diaries and letters with their later recollections in their autobiographies.

Such documents also vary regardless of their categorisation as diaries, letters or autobiographies, but depending on the personal factors involved in their production. The author may be inexperienced or an expert witness, may have limited powers of expression or a vivid memory for detail, may be tired or refreshed when writing the account, may be in a rush or have plenty of time, may be staking a claim for themselves or be emotionally detached from the issues involved. All such aspects require careful assessment when the researcher is evaluating the source. Again, there are opportunities here for judging rival accounts of the same event produced by different individuals involved, whatever the form of their chosen method of expression.

Diaries

The modern diary form originated in the sixteenth century, apparently a product of a growth of individual self-awareness. According to Arthur Ponsonby, in his classic study of English diaries, 'The idea of writing down daily thoughts and notes on passing events, especially when it takes a more or less introspective form, is of comparatively modern growth, and would seem to be the outcome of the increasing self-consciousness which intellectual development has produced in humanity' (Ponsonby 1923, p. 3).

Diarists are preoccupied with their own subjective responses to events (Tosh 2002, p. 72), and in recording these express contemporary sensibilities and impressions at the level of individual consciousness (Fothergill 1974, p. 12).

The potential value of the diary as a documentary source has often been emphasised. To Ponsonby, it is their expression of 'human nature – our own nature' that is significant and indeed unique to diaries. As he observes,

> We can enter into the trivial pleasures and petty miseries of daily life – the rainy day, the blunt razor, the new suit, the domestic quarrel, the bad night, the twinge of toothache, the fall from a horse, the newly purchased book, the good meal, the over-sharp criticism, the irritating relation, the child's maladies, the exasperating servant. We know them all. We have experienced many of them.
>
> (Ponsonby 1923, p. 32)

Moreover, he adds,

> Notwithstanding all the immense store of facts we are compiling by means of newspapers, books, registers and official records with regard to the history of our own times, the privately written comments of an individual spontaneously scribbled and so reproducing the mood, the atmosphere, and, so to speak, the particular aroma of the moment, are priceless and can be regarded as the spice of history.
>
> (Ponsonby 1923, p. 43)

Fothergill is no less enthusiastic:

> They were so concretely *there*, so firmly embedded in the centre of their own existences, each consciousness composing all the elements of its experience into a unique and incommunicable set of relations, with itself as the focal point of the world. One's sense of the substance of history is turned inside out. Where one habitually thought of 'ordinary lives' forming a vast background to historical 'events', now one's vision is of the great events daily passing behind the immediate realities that comprise an individual's experience.
>
> (Fothergill 1974, p. 9)

It is this immediacy of the record of everyday experience that makes diaries a key source for historians and social researchers.

Diaries provide valuable evidence of women's lives as well as those of men. Harriet Blodgett's work on Englishwomen's private diaries since the sixteenth century stresses their subjective character, but also demonstrates how they express what women have taken to be true about themselves and their world (Blodgett 1988, p. 18). In the case of women, diaries have represented a means of self-expression undistorted by external influences or public expectations in a patriarchal culture. Nevertheless, they are often reticent about the most intimate details of their lives, for example about sex. Such reticence may well hamper the researcher. It is also important to judge the accuracy and credibility of accounts offered in diaries, just as in any other source, and to gauge where the diarist may be embroidering, exaggerating or even fabricating reality.

There are several factors involved in diary writing that may affect their value for researchers. One of these is the frequency of entries, and especially whether the diarist records events soon after they take place, perhaps on a daily basis, or after a longer period has elapsed. Ponsonby points out that there is a major difference between a daily diary and one that is written up every few days or longer: 'The impulsive note of the moment catches a mood and picks up an impression which may in twenty-four hours evaporate and which in a week or month will have entirely disappeared' (Ponsonby 1923, p. 4). This is not a matter of the accuracy of the record made, for an immediate entry can be so caught up in the heat of the moment that it loses its balance, whereas a later entry may be cooler and more dispassionate. However, the small details are more likely to be evoked soon after the event, as is the unresolved nature of the problems involved. The diarist who is relating events more or less as they are taking place does not know their outcome, and therefore cannot use hindsight to assess their significance, as is the case with someone who waits for the dust to settle.

It is not always easy to judge exactly when a diary entry has been written and what its relation is to the event being described, especially as diarists are not always consistent in their practices. For instance, the diary of John Evelyn in the seventeenth century is a confusing mixture of diary and memoir, with further details and clarifications often added long after the original event or entry (Ponsonby 1933, chapter 7). In the case of the twentieth-century Labour Party politician Richard Crossman, entries were made weekly, reflecting on the incidents and issues of each day of the previous week, often with the help of notes and minutes. Crossman himself acknowledged that his aim was to 'keep a record of the transient impressions of politics as they are made on one personality', in order for him to note, 'before they are forgotten, opinions which are proved wrong and judgments which one would rather not have made'. This, he felt, was more difficult after a fortnight had elapsed, because 'one tends to telescope events into conformity with one's present interests and so to distort or improve the path' (Morgan 1981, p. 13, quoting Crossman's diary entry of 24 March 1954). According to the editor of his diary, Janet Morgan, Crossman looked over his account only rarely, 'since he was anxious to avoid tinkering with his own prose and wished to set out his opinions of the current week undefiled by the memory of his earlier prognostications' (Morgan 1981, p. 15).

The motivation behind the diary is a further issue that needs to be taken into account when evaluating it for research purposes. It may be for oneself, as a guide or a record for the future. In some such cases, Fothergill suggests, it can become a 'Book of the Self', developing an overall whole that reflects the writer's life, or a 'serial autobiography' (Fothergill 1974, p. 154). In other cases, it is intended for publication, that is, it is deliberately written in order for others to read. Crossman, himself a political scientist and journalist as well as a leading politician of his day, was explicitly concerned to set out a day-to-day account of the internal controversies of the Labour Party that would be of use for historians. When he became a government Minister in 1964, he realised as he recalled later that 'if I could achieve a continuous record of my whole Ministerial life, dictated while the memory was still hot and uncontaminated by "improvements", this part of the diary would become of quite special historical value' (Crossman 1975, p. 12). After thinking at first of using this mainly as raw material for a book, he then saw that the diary itself would be of more interest as a 'daily picture' of the life of a Cabinet Minister, including 'exactly what he did in his Department, in Cabinet Committee and in Cabinet itself, and how much official time he spent outside his office visiting authorities under his control, and finally what he had left for his family at the weekend' (Crossman 1975, p. 12). Thus, he sums up his aims in writing and publishing his diary of these years:

> if I could publish a diary of my years as a Minister without any Minis-
> terial improvements, as a true record of how one Minister thought and
> felt, I would have done something towards lighting up the secret
> places of British politics and enabling any intelligent elector to have a
> picture of what went on behind the scenes between 1964 and 1970.
>
> (Crossman 1975, p. 12)

He concedes that his account is 'neither objective nor fair', even though 'as a lifelong political scientist I have tried to discipline myself to objectivity'. It had to be 'one-sided and immensely partisan', he insists, in order for it to be 'true to life' (Crossman 1975, p. 13).

It would be possible to propose three broad categories of diaries: private, political and official. Private diaries are concerned especially to record one's own development, for one's own satisfaction. Political diaries, of the kind pioneered by Crossman and which have burgeoned ever since, are mainly designed to give the inside story on public events, for the interest of others. Official diaries are kept as a requirement of one's position in an institution, such as a ship's log by the captain of the vessel. There are significant differences of emphasis and function between these three basic types. However, all of these forms of diary may be of use in helping to reveal aspects both of the 'private' and of the 'public'.

The diary of Samuel Pepys from 1660 to 1669, generally regarded as one of the greatest of all diaries, might be seen as a personal diary. It was written daily, was scrupulously honest in dealing with his own faults and foibles, and was not intended for publication. It is filled with intimate details about his life and personal relationships, especially with his wife, Elizabeth, and his several mistresses. Indeed, the first daily entry, for 1 January 1660, gives some sense of this: 'This morning (we lying lately in the garret) I rose, put on my suit with great skirts, having not lately worn any other clothes but them . . . Dined at home in the garret, where my wife dressed the remains of a turkey, and in the doing of it she burned her hand' (Latham and Matthews 1970, p. 3; entry for 1 January 1660). At the same time, it provides a first-hand account of major public events such as the Restoration of Charles II to the English throne in 1660, the Great Plague of 1665, and the great Fire of London the following year. Pepys was also himself involved in public life in his post at the Navy in which he was to become highly successful. According to his most recent biographer, Claire Tomalin, 'He intended from the first to cover public events but also made it clear from the first page that it was to be a chronicle of intimate experience' (Tomalin 2003, p. 83). Thus, his diary offers significant insights on both his private affairs and public matters of state, or, as the editors of the diary argue, 'both an individual's experience and the multiple experiences of his society' (Latham and Matthews 1970, p. cxv). The boundaries between the 'public chronicle' and the 'private journal' become blurred in Pepys's diary, to the extent that

> Because the diary tells an historical story in terms of an individual life, the reader is given not only an intellectual understanding of the period but also the means of achieving an imaginative sympathy with it. Reader and subject are united by a common humanity. This is not only one man's version of the history of a decade – this is what it felt like to be alive.
>
> (Latham and Matthews 1970, p. cxxxvii)

In the case of the political diary, as Crossman showed, the witness testimony is about public life, or what it is like to be involved in great events that affect society as a whole. This for example is Crossman's account of a meeting of the British Cabinet on 10 August 1966, which he attended as Secretary of State for Housing before being moved to be Lord President of the Council in a summer reshuffle of Cabinet positions:

> By the time Cabinet met at 11.45 I knew that the appointments would be announced that night, that we had to be at Buckingham Palace on

Thursday morning to be sworn in, and that we were also to have our first meeting of the new Economic Strategy Committee. Meanwhile, I started the morning at the Social Services Committee, working on the new pensions scheme, and thinking about my future. The Cabinet went in a perfectly normal way. The Chancellor made it clear that, despite the cuts already announced, he wanted the PESC exercise to be carried through, cutting back all departmental estimates from 11 and a half to 4 and a half per cent. I said we couldn't consider that request unless we knew what the total deflation packet was. How much will consumption be cut by last week's package? How much will S.E.T. cut consumption when it comes into force in October? Harold [Wilson, the Prime Minister] replied by at last giving his priorities for expenditure. Number one, expenditure designed to increase industrial productivity; number two, our three public works programmes – housing, education and hospitals; number three, social security and social services; number four, individual consumption. What we can't commit ourselves to are expanded programmes of pensions, which blow up consumption. If we'd thought of it, added Harold, we would never have abolished prescription charges, but in those days we were young and inexperienced. Instead, we would have cut back school meals, which cost us £120 million.

(Crossman 1975, p. 607)

Tony Benn, a fellow diarist who was recording the events of a Labour Cabinet from his own Ministerial position when Crossman's diaries were published in 1976, was duly appreciative: 'They throw a light on politics as it really is and say nothing malicious that hasn't appeared in every newspaper journalist's articles about the Cabinet for years. But coming from Dick it has a certain authenticity' (Benn 1990, p. 638, entry for 7 November 1976). At a deeper level, such accounts also offer many of the features of the private diary, transferred to the public stage. They give intimacy and detail, all the more interesting for being indiscreet. They give freshness and immediacy, often revealing as much about the author as about the event being discussed. At the same time, they give an insight into the miscalculations of the moment, and provide additional point to Ponsonby's remark about the writer's 'ignorance of the morrow' (Ponsonby 1933, p. 182).

Diaries are often personal and political at the same time, strikingly so in the case of Frances Stevenson, official secretary as well as the mistress of the British Prime Minister David Lloyd George in the early twentieth century. It is a fascinating source on the character and politics of Lloyd George, although, as the historian A.J.P. Taylor points out, it is important to be wary of the limitations of the record, with regard to both his political and his private affairs:

> What Frances Stevenson records is often second-hand. She does not tell us what happened in cabinet, and it is therefore not surprising that he usually came out best. The Diary is very much Lloyd George's version of events. The same is true of his private life. Naturally he worked off on Frances Stevenson the irritation which he sometimes felt with his family. It does not follow that they were as tiresome as he made out or as she was led to believe.
>
> (Taylor 1971, p. x)

Another aspect of this diary, as with many others, is that it is inconsistent in its coverage, as she was sometimes either too busy or too tired to write entries, and it might lapse for weeks or months at a time. At one point, as Taylor notes, the diary does not take the negotiations with the Irish in 1921 to their conclusion, even though Frances Stevenson was apparently waiting in an anteroom when the treaty was being signed (Taylor 1971, p. xi).

Political diaries are also able to shed light on the diarist's private or social life, which is rarely far away from public considerations. For instance, Crossman notes as follows on spending a weekend at King's College, Cambridge, in May 1956:

> It was exquisite, early summer weather for strolling along the Backs and in the Trinity Fellows' garden, full of flowering trees, or for sitting on Nicky Kaldor's lawn just behind, while the children played with hoops, or for walking over the flat country and through the bluebell woods. The Kahn-Kaldor-Robinson set are all keen Socialists but somehow they are detached from practical politics. On the other hand, they curiously succeed in giving one the impression that they care about what one's doing, and mind, which is a nice consoling pillow on which to lay one's head.
>
> (Crossman 1981, p. 229; entry for 13 May 1956)

This mixture of the public and private is if anything even more evident in more recent political diaries such as those of Tony Benn and Alan Clark. Benn's diary provides a running commentary on politics and society in Britain from the Second World War period (Benn 1995) to the early twenty-first century (Benn 2002), from the perspective of a left-wing activist and Labour politician. The original transcript of his diary for the period 1973–6 alone apparently amounts to 1,750,000 words in total, of which 325,000 were published in the relevant collection (Benn 1990). Benn's account of the origins of the so-called 'Great Debate' on education in October 1976 under James Callaghan as the Labour Prime Minister and Shirley Williams as Secretary of State for education and science reveals key tensions and differences over comprehensive education. It also sheds light on the nature of his relationship with his wife, Caroline, an active supporter of comprehensive schools. In so doing, it draws on the experience of policy changes in education over the previous thirty years (see Case Study 6).

Case Study 6

Tony Benn and the 'Great Debate' on education, September–October 1976
Based on Benn's published diary (Benn 1990), pp. 609–29

Friday 10 September
There is going to be a reshuffle triggered off by Roy Jenkins who has finally left the Government. Merlyn Rees becomes Home Secretary; Shirley [Williams] is diverted into Education where she will have to carry the can on all the public expenditure cuts (although she does fully support them); John Silkin has been kept in, which surprised me, to become Minister of Agriculture, and there are three new members of the Cabinet – Roy Hattersley, Stan Orme and Bill Rodgers. Fred Peart is now Leader of the Lords – how he survives, I don't know . . .

Thursday 30 September
We went over to the [Labour Party] Conference and the first item was on education. Caroline's name was mentioned several times by one speaker who kept quoting 'Benn and Simon', i.e. the book Caroline co-authored *Halfway There*. The Socialist Education Association delegate spoke and attacked the quality of comprehensive education, which is part of the ultra-left campaign, and will be used by the *Daily Mail* no doubt . . .

Tuesday 12 October
It is 2 am and today is Caroline's birthday. We have had such a marvellous life together and her radicalism and support and determination have really kept me going. I couldn't have managed without her . . .

Thursday 14 October
Cabinet at 10. I asked Shirley about the reports that Jim [Callaghan] is going to make a major education speech and she passed me a note saying, 'Tony, no question of any change in emphasis on comprehensives. It's mainly on maths, why not enough kids are doing engineering, etc. A bit about standards. Curriculum will be the main row.' Caroline

continued on next page

---

thinks it is to root out the 'lefties' who are teaching the social sciences, and all that. Shirley must be a bit worried, when the PM makes a speech on her subject . . .

Monday 18 October
Jim Callaghan's speech on education is all over the news. It has opened up the debate on the future of education in a way most damaging to the cause of comprehensive education, and the Tory papers have gone to town over it. After years of inactive Education secretaries, we now have in Shirley Williams a right-wing one working with a Prime Minister who has allowed himself to be briefed by Department of Education officials who themselves don't use the state system and who are hostile to it . . .

Thursday 21 October
I have been trying to get hold of the memorandum prepared by Department of Education and Science officials for the PM in connection with his speech on education. It was leaked to *The Times Educational Supplement*. Jim, in fairness, just suggested that we should have a national debate but he and Shirley are working hand-in-glove to introduce reactionary education policies. My office rang Shirley's office, but they wouldn't send it to me. In Cabinet Shirley said to me, 'I'll let you have it, it was Number 10 [Downing Street, home of the Prime Minister] that was the trouble.'

I said, 'If it can be leaked to the press, I think another Cabinet Minister is entitled to see it.'

She is worried because she knows she is engaged in some shifty change of policy and she has got all the teachers up in arms. Ironically, the press is building her up as the best Education Secretary, saying that she has inherited Roy Jenkins's mantle, etc . . .

Monday 25 October
During the TUC-Labour Party Liaison Committee, Jim said, 'I will just briefly report on my education speech. We may need a core curriculum; to talk about the three Rs can't be reactionary. We should be thinking about education and employment in engineering, about exams, and possibly publish a Green [consultative] paper.'

Len Murray [TUC president] welcomed the PM's speech, but said that education was not training. We could look at the curriculum but perhaps we should be looking at higher education, which had unfilled vacancies. We needed to attract more mature students.

continued on facing page

I welcomed the fact that the debate had been opened by the Prime Minister because there was a massive attack on our comprehensive schools and we had to reject it. 'There are certain dangers to face: the danger of divisiveness engendered by the 1944 Education Act with all its nonsense about different types of minds requiring different types of schools, resurrected by Sir Cyril Burt who has, incidentally, been accused in *The Sunday Times* of doing fraudulent research into intelligence.

'The second danger is the binary system of higher education and the third is exams which we have talked about for ten years, whereby working-class kids get CSEs [Certificate of Secondary Education] and others get GCEs [General Certificate of Education]. We must turn away completely from the idea that working class kids should be given technical training and shunted into industry. We have to deal with the massive subsidies to private education, and we must end the stranglehold of universities over the school exam.'

I had prepared this little speech with Caroline's help, and Shirley sat there blushing, pink as anything, and I think I scored a lot of direct hits on what she would like to bring forward.

Shirley then warned against a backlash. There were genuine concerns about teaching methods: fashions in teaching had changed and hadn't always been thought through. We must look at the basics again and at the big comprehensives and avoid the mistakes of the past. In the sixteen to nineteen age groups there was duplication of provision which we couldn't afford. We could save hundreds of thousands of pounds. On higher education, we needed a gap between school and university. The polytechnics were dropping their part-timers, and student grants might perhaps only be payable to those who had previously worked.

Clark's is also a highly successful political diary, but he describes all diaries as 'intensely personal', and suggests that to publish them is 'a baring, if not a flaunting, of the ego' (Clark 1994, p. xi). He insists that his diaries 'are not written to throw light on events in the past, or retrospectively to justify the actions of the author', but are, rather, '*exactly* as they were recorded on the day; sometimes even the hour, or the minute, of a particular episode or sensation' (Clark 1994, p. xi). His first published collection of diaries covers a period, 1983–91, when he is a Minister in three successive British Conservative governments, but he notes that fewer than half of the entries in it are devoted to the themes that dominated political life during this time (Clark 1994, p. xi). Like Benn, he apparently kept a diary from his youth, originally without expecting them to be published. In Clark's case there is rarely any visible partition between private and the public life, especially as he is continually preoccupied with his own physical appearance and the rise and fall of his own political fortunes (see also Clark 2001).

The third general type of diary, the log book, contains a great deal of basic information about a specific institution that is maintained on an ongoing basis. In the case of a school log book, for example, it would usually include changes in pupil numbers from year to year, staff changes, and the dates of formal school inspections. In some instances, they also record the experience of administering the institution, and the problems and frustrations that are involved in this may be noted in a very personal way. For example, Brinsley G. Edwards, the headmaster of Wolverhampton Technical High School, kept a highly detailed log book that sheds much light on the changing relationship between the school and its LEA. As the relationship deteriorated towards the end of 1958, and following a set of poor examination results for the school, Edwards was called to a meeting at the LEA, and noted in his log book the 'very discouraging' approach of the officials: 'Further I was not given a copy of the statistics – they each had a copy! In the last four years I find it hard to recall any compliment paid to the school or to secondary technical education by this trio of officials' (Wolverhampton THS log book, 14 November 1958). The attack was continued at the next meeting of the school governors, when, according to Edwards, 'No good points were given the slightest praise but weaknesses were probed carefully' (Wolverhampton THS log book, 20 November 1958. See also McCulloch 1989, pp. 142–6). Thus, while such a document will have a formal and official function, it may again reveal the daily detail of life, and the hopes and failures of humanity.

Letters

Unlike the keeping of diaries, letter writing is an ancient social practice, familiar in the earliest literate societies both as a means of maintaining bureaucratic control and for the exchange of personal information (Earle 1999, p. 1). In the early modern and more recent periods, huge numbers have been produced. The archive of the Verney family in Buckinghamshire over twelve generations from the 1630s to the mid eighteenth century contains over thirty thousand personal letters written during this period. Letter writing was a badge of membership in elite society, obeying the conventions of politeness as well as dynastic and individual needs (Whyman 1999, p. 19). In the nineteenth century, the use of trains and ships, together with cheaper postage, encouraged even wider and more frequent circulation of letters, and soon also of postcards. In Britain, following the introduction of Rowland Hill's penny post in 1840, the number of chargeable letters per year increased from about 75 million to 196 million within two years, and by the end of the decade it had reached 329 million (Secord 2000, p. 29). In the United States, the first postal stamps were issued in 1853, and the number of items carried doubled to 7.4 billion between 1886 and 1901 (Briggs and Burke 2002, p. 133).

During the Second World War, it has been estimated that in all probability more letters were written, posted, lost and recovered than at any other time before or since. Letter writing was often the only form of communication possible in war conditions, whether over short or long distances. Between March 1944 and March 1945, the one-way traffic of letters sent overseas from Britain reached 374 million (Hartley 1999, p. 183). Over the past century, rival forms of communications such as the telephone have eroded the primacy of letters. Indeed, in the last decade the rise of electronic mail has eclipsed what has come to be known rather derisively as snail-mail. Nevertheless, letters comprise a massive and still continuing type of documentary evidence that is rich in potential significance for social researchers and historians.

A further difference between letters and diaries is that letters are essentially interactive between the writer and the intended recipient. They are fashioned in order to make sense to one person, or in some cases a group of people, rather than anyone else, so as to convey information to them alone. This information may be in the form of a story or a warning; it may be short or long and rambling; it may be written all at one time or over a period. Plummer goes so far as to suggest that 'Letters are not generally focused enough to be of analytic interest – they contain far too much material that strays from the researcher's concern' (Plummer 2001, p. 55). A letter may also be a response to a previous letter or sequence of letters, either from the recipient or from other sources, and so needs to be related to these earlier documents, potentially a network of correspondence rather than simply a set of exchanges between two people, in order to be fully understood.

Letters are commonly categorised as 'private' correspondence, between members of the same family for example, and 'public' or 'official' correspondence for the purposes of business or bureaucracy. Marwick stresses that 'An official letter sent by a foreign secretary will contain different kinds of information, and will need different types of analysis, from a private letter sent by the same foreign secretary to his wife [*sic*], which may, in some circumstances, actually contain more frank, and more usable, information' (Marwick 2001, p. 181). Nevertheless, such a categorisation can be misleading. Rebecca Earle confronts this issue directly: 'why should we expect letters to maintain a rigorous distinction between the personal and the public? The boundary is scarcely clear in economic and social realms; the desire for clear epistolary demarcation into public and private represents an attempt to impose an artificial clarity' (Earle 1999, p. 4). The boundaries between the private and the public are blurred in letters as in other documentary sources, and there are many crossing points.

Lloyd George's letters to his secretary and mistress Frances Stevenson exemplify this duality, as their editor A.J.P. Taylor notes:

> Reading these letters, there can be no doubting the sincerity of his love. But even in love Lloyd George was still the adroit politician whose magic was exercised on the Allies, the Irish, the Irish, the Bolsheviks, and of course on the British people. His letters were skilfully tuned to Frances's nature. After protestations of love, he would turn to great affairs, initiate her into state secrets and – most skilful of all – appeal for her advice. No doubt he welcomed her advice, but he also knew that Frances was flattered to be asked to give it. His words were calculated even when he was most in earnest.
>
> (Taylor 1975, pp. vii–viii)

Letters of an especially personal type might well be exchanged between spouses and partners, especially when they are separated either for a long period or for a specific purpose such as a journey. Even in such cases, gossip and endearments might well be mixed with general reflections and items of business. For example, a letter from Cyril Norwood to his fiancée Catherine in November 1901 shortly before their wedding includes preparations for the marriage, descriptions of some of the wedding presents, arrangements for their house, a discussion of problems in his own family, comments on a forthcoming school concert and a final declaration of personal sincerity and commitment. On his family problems, Norwood comments frankly:

> I think my father is very cut up about the wedding, but I think it will do him good. He was very glib about the defalcation he had committed, and didn't seem to think that he had done anything special. He probably doesn't, and regards himself as a man upon whom much trouble has come, and whose life is made barren. He never seems to recognise that it is he who by his own agency has made his own life barren.

Then the mood lightens, but still Norwood is conveying information albeit couched in pleasantries:

> Well, darling, only four weeks and a bit more, and the time is simply racing by with me. I doubt whether I shall get that house into anything like right, but I am getting a lot of help. Kelsey and Stockdale are awfully good. The place will want a lot of airing, and the bedding will have to be simply baked for a couple of days. I wish these four weeks and a bit were over and that I was away in the Isle of Wight with you: how I look forward to our married life sweetheart! I feel as if I was

just going to draw out of the troubled water into the quiet: I know we shall be very happy.

(Cyril Norwood to Catherine Kilner, 17 November 1901;
Norwood papers, University of Sheffield)

Thomas and Znaniecki, in their classic study *The Polish Peasant*, suggest that family letters are 'naïve and unreflective' (Thomas and Znaniecki 1918–20/1927, vol. 2, p. 1123). Norwood's letter does not bear this out, and in fact despite their often rambling and shifting styles a great number of significant issues are often raised in such documents, and clues offered that the recipient will be expected to pick up. The researcher needs to be especially alert to coded messages and hints in this kind of letter.

As one would expect, there is an obvious contrast to be drawn between Norwood's letters to his fiancée and his correspondence with his LEA in his capacity as a head teacher. Letters in the latter category are formal or official in nature, stiff in their politeness. They are designed to be placed on record and discussed by officials and committees in the interests of the school's further development. For example, as Head of Bristol Grammar School in 1911, Norwood wrote to the Bristol Education Committee to ask for an increase of its annual grant to the school. His letter included a detailed case for additional income for the school and showed how it would be put to good use. He concluded:

I anticipate in consequence a period of rising expenditure, and while I hope that income will also tend to increase, we have to remember that the endowment has now to be spread over a much great number of boys. I believe the School capable of greater expansion, and because it is open to every class in the City I heartily and confidently think it worthy of increased support to enable it to fulfil its full functions in every direction. I shall not be satisfied unless the School is able to give the best of education in every branch of Secondary School work up to the highest limit of age, but to do this we shall need money, and therefore I put this claim before you with hope.

(Cyril Norwood, letter to Bristol Education Committee, 8 June 1911;
Bristol Grammar School board of governors meeting, 9 June 1911,
minute book no. 3, Bristol Records Office, Bristol)

In this case, Norwood's letter had a dual function as it was tabled for discussion at a meeting of the school's board of governors. Norwood was thus able to press his case for further resources while at the same time making sure that his underlying aims and objectives for the school were clearly understood and noted. This kind of official correspondence is widely used, but it is important to recognise the purposes and audiences involved in order to gauge its full significance.

There are many letters that do not fit straightforwardly into a typology of 'personal' and 'formal'. For example, correspondents to newspapers and public institutions are often expressing their own private concerns, whether for public record or for official action. The letter from a parent to the Minister of Education in New Zealand has already been discussed above (Case Study 4). Christine Heward has also analysed in depth an archive of letters sent by parents of pupils to the Headmaster of an English public school, Ellesmere College, between 1929 and 1950. According to Heward,

> These letters demonstrate, with simple candour, the concerns of a small group of parents in bringing up their sons; what their aspirations were, their plans, fears and problems. They help us to understand what they wanted for their sons' futures, how they attempted to realise their aspirations, why they sent their sons to a public school and what the alternatives were.
>
> (Heward 1988, p. ix)

This source, comprising 180 files of correspondence from parents to the school, provides evidence of 'the ways in which a small group of parents sought to bring up their sons and planned their education and careers' (Heward 1988, p. 14). Different groups of parents are also analysed and compared from the evidence of these letters. Widows and the clergy tended to write 'begging letters' – the former detailing their own family circumstances, the latter waxing lyrical on a wide range of religious and educational issues. Farmers, on the other hand, wrote little and were usually brief when they did so. Overall, this correspondence sheds light on the interaction between the personal or family domain and the concerns of an established social institution, revealing a great deal about the concerns that they had in common, and also about the ambitions, fears and anxieties which played themselves out in different ways.

Beyond this, there is a further class of letters that might perhaps be best described as political in character. These are written from one person to another, but not generally within the same family and increasingly not even within the same country or society. They engage in small talk, but tend to be polite rather than intimate in character. They may well be related to specific institutions, but are not official representations of the institution. They may ramble, but they have a particular point, to persuade the recipient to take a particular action, or to desist from one, or to support a particular line. Two letters illustrate this kind of letter, both written to the political scientist and left-wing activist Harold Laski in the 1940s. The first is by Victor Gollancz, a leading publisher of the time and the originator of the Left Book Club in 1936. The second is by Clement Attlee, the leader of the Labour Party, who became Prime Minister following Labour's general election victory in 1945.

Gollancz's letter to Laski was designed to encourage him to be more sympathetic to left-wing activities outside the orbit of the Labour Party, such as were being developed by other radical figures such as J.B. Priestley and Sir Richard Acland. Laski was frustrated by the lack of vigour being shown by Labour, which was part of the wartime Coalition government, but was suspicious that splinter groups would exacerbate left-wing divisions. In his letter, Gollancz tries to develop a workable way forward to enhance the political prospects of the Left. First, he recounts his areas of agreement and disagreement with Laski. For example, he points out,

> The following is where we differ. You feel that the tactic of trying to persuade the Party to leave the Government if the banks, the land and the mines have not been nationalised within X months will result in the weakening of the monopolists and in the first step to power, whereas I think that it will have the opposite effect. I don't think it can possibly 'come off'. It is, of course, often the right thing to press a scheme that won't come off, because as a result of pressing it you get, not what you are pressing for, but something; but this doesn't happen if you are pressing for something which everybody knows in advance you won't get. This is what I think about this tactic.

Instead, Gollancz, argues, Laski should adopt a different approach:

> The alternative tactic that I want to propose is to press in every sort of way – at the [Labour Party] conference, through the press that is friendly to us, through the Labour members of the Left Book Club groups, and so on – for the ending of the electoral truce. Here is a demand which arises out of the immediate situation and corresponds, I believe overwhelmingly, with the desires of Labour people everywhere. I believe that if you proposed this at the conference every man would rise in his place and cheer you to the echo. And I believe that after a very short campaign there would be such an overwhelming pressure on Transport House [the then headquarters of the Labour Party] that they would find it impossible to resist.
>
> (Victor Gollancz to Harold Laski, 8 May 1942;
> copy in Kingsley Martin archive, Sussex University Library, file 29/7;
> reproduced in full in McCulloch 1982)

Like political diaries, this kind of letter has an immediacy that makes it possible to gauge the expectations, and the miscalculations, operating in a particular context. In this case, Gollancz proved to have miscalculated somewhat, as a resolution to end the electoral truce was defeated at the Labour Party Conference at the end of May 1942, if only narrowly (*Labour Party Conference Report* 1942, p. 150). It is important not to assume that what is claimed in such documents is necessarily accurate, and they are very often imbued with bias about issues and other people that should be understood and taken into account when evaluating them.

The second letter, from Clement Attlee, has a rather different tone. It is friendly and familiar on the surface, but whereas Gollancz seeks to flatter and persuade, Attlee's purpose is to rebuke and criticise. It is written in August 1945, soon after Attlee has taken office as Prime Minister and during Laski's one-year term as the chairman of the Labour Party's national executive committee. Laski has been using his position to try to force the hand of the new Labour Government in a number of directions, and Attlee is writing to stop him from doing so (Clement Attlee to Harold Laski, 20 August 1945; in Laski papers, Hull University Library, file 13)

> My dear Harold,
> Your letter has just reached me and I hope you will make useful contacts in the Scandinavian countries. I thank you also for your kindly reference in your Reynolds article [in the newspaper *Reynolds News*]. I am however bound to point out to you that the constant flow of speeches from and interviews with you are embarrassing. I replied to [Winston] Churchill [the Leader of the Opposition] that you had, of course, a perfect right to speak as an individual but that your speeches did not commit the Government.
> Nevertheless as Chairman of the Labour Party Executive, you hold an important office in the Party and the position is not well understood abroad. Your utterances are taken to express the views of the Government.
> In yesterday's Daily Telegraph you are reported to have said in a signed interview in La Tribune Economique, 'the Labour Government would if necessary bring economic pressure to bear on Spain'. If you made a statement in this form, you are seriously at fault. You have no right whatever to speak on behalf of the Government. Foreign Affairs are in the capable hands of Ernest Bevin. His task is quite sufficiently difficult without the embarrassment of irresponsible statements of the kind which you are making.
> I had hoped to have seen you but you were away in Paris. I can assure you there is widespread resentment in the Party at your activities and a period of silence on your part would be welcome.
> Yours ever,
>
> Clem.

Attlee was in fact an acknowledged master of this kind of letter. A year before, he had acknowledged a long letter from Laski inviting him to resign as Labour Party leader with the briefest of replies: 'Dear Laski, thank you for your letter, contents of which have been noted' (quoted in Kramnick and Sheerman 1993, p. 481). This letter imitated the terse business reply, just as his letter of August 1945 had similarities with an intimate personal letter ('My dear Harold . . . yours ever, Clem'), but both are public and political in their deeper substance. Such documents are potentially valuable for researchers of politics and society, and deserve rather greater attention alongside the current preoccupation with political diaries.

Autobiographies

Autobiography, the telling of the story of one's own life, is probably the commonest type of personal document. The earliest recognised example of an autobiography is St Augustine's *Confessions*, in *c*. A.D. 400, and the term itself was not invented until the nineteenth century, but over the past four hundred years they have become highly popular forms of self-expression. As Allport wryly observed, 'Gradually the flood increased until now we have an annual torrent of backward glances, stories of one's own life, pilgrims' ways, reminiscences, voyages, recollections' (Allport 1947, p. 76). This gathering avalanche has involved a broadening of the types of individuals who have committed their life stories to paper. The elite, the rich and the famous may still be the most conspicuous authors of autobiographies, but they have been joined by many ordinary people, men and women, offering their versions of life as they have lived it (Plummer 2001, p. 95).

The attraction of the autobiography is that it offers an opportunity to look back over one's life and the lessons that it holds. As several commentators have emphasised, it is essentially an inside account of the progress made during a lifetime, and the pitfalls encountered, mistakes made and opportunities taken and missed along the way. According to Allport, 'The great merit of an autobiography is that it gives the "inside half" of the life; the half that is hidden from the objectively-minded scientist' (Allport 1947, p. 77). Burgess endorses this judgement, pointing out that an autobiography provides 'an *insider's* point of view' (Burgess 1984a, p. 126). Similarly, Tosh notes that 'Their fascination derives from the fact that they are the recollections of an insider' (Tosh 2002, p. 61). Such recollections, moreover, embrace a very wide variety in terms of human experience, as Vincent observes: 'The infinite variation in the patterns of occupational and family life, and in the forms and fortunes of attempts at self-improvement and self-expression which are to be found in these works serve as a necessary reminder that the shared experience of particular material and ideological forces did not produce identical life-histories' (Vincent 1981, pp. 198–9). There may therefore be no such thing as a 'representative' autobiography, except in so far as each is a contribution to an understanding of the teeming variety of human life. The autobiography is therefore potentially an important source of evidence for historians and social researchers. Nevertheless, it is subject to a number of problems in terms of interpretation that require some care. Moreover, even though its primary focus of attention may be the individual self, its bearing on social and public issues again merits elaboration and emphasis.

Autobiographies differ from diaries and letters principally in that they are written usually long after the developments they appraise. This is both an advantage and a disadvantage in terms of their potential use as a documentary source. It is helpful, first of all, because they can provide a considered judgement on past events, with what is usually regarded as the wisdom of hindsight. It is problematic because the accounts they give are not impartial and also due to the effects of memory. Personal bias is a trait that is especially associated with diaries and letters, but it is not necessarily less of a factor when passion is spent. On the contrary, the autobiography can serve to justify and rationalise the decisions taken during one's life. Tosh warns us that, in general, 'the author's purpose is less to offer an objective account than to justify his or her actions in retrospect and to provide evidence for the defence before the bar of history'. Indeed, Tosh insists, 'Autobiographies may be very revealing of mentality and values, but as a record of events they are often inaccurate and selective to the point of deception' (Tosh 2002, p. 61).

There is a further sense in which autobiographies cannot be regarded as 'representative', which is that their subjects constitute a relatively small and atypical group of individuals. John Burnett regards this as the chief defect in the use of autobiographies, as well as of diaries: 'To keep a daily journal or to write the story of one's life is, and was, at once atypical, especially for working people to whom writing did not usually come easily' (Burnett 1974, p. 11). The motivation of the author is an especially important consideration in these circumstances in appraising the value of autobiographies. Some are written to pass the time, or to keep for reference or for the family. Although these have no commercial purpose, they will still tend to paint the author in a flattering light, if only for his or her *amour propre*. Others are written for publication, which means that they may emphasise conflicts, controversies and scandals for the sake of increasing potential interest and sales. At the same time, publication entails some regard being given to laws of libel, obscenity and literary standards, and also means that there is an opportunity for the account to be debated and challenged in public (Allport 1947, p. 77).

Moreover, the autobiography tends to seek to impose a pattern, even a general purpose, on the many different spheres and dimensions of a life. Roy Pascal argues that, in its shaping of the past, the autobiography 'imposes a pattern on a life, constructs out of it a coherent story' (Pascal 1960, p. 9). Indeed, he continues, the realisation of a 'meaningful standpoint, the emergence from shadows into daylight', is itself 'a condition of autobiography altogether' (Pascal 1960, p. 10). This means that the autobiography entails a discernible storyline, in which unlike the diary or the letter the end of the story is already evident. There may still be surprises in store for the author, as in the case of the academic and former politician H.A.L. Fisher, who optimistically entitled his life story *An Unfinished Autobiography*, which had to be published posthumously after he was knocked over and killed by a motor vehicle (Ogg 1947, p. 141). Nevertheless, the writing of such a work demands committing oneself to a plot and subplots, which usually means that some aspects are magnified, while others are played down or left on the cutting-room floor.

In this process of editing a life, whether consciously or unconsciously, the role of memory becomes a significant issue. Some incidents are forgotten, especially from infancy and early childhood, but such amnesia can be selective in nature. For example, the autobiography of John Major, the former British Prime Minister, somehow overlooked a liaison with Edwina Currie, one of his Cabinet ministers; an omission that she rectified in her own published diaries (Major 2000; Currie 2002). In many cases, too, the complexities of events are reduced to bare outlines, or may be rendered as simple and often misleading summaries. Thus, as Allport acknowledges, an autobiographer is not fully aware of his or her own life story. In an unconsciously gendered image, Allport contends that 'what he knows he may dress up, prettify, before exposing it to view' (Allport 1947, p. 77). In other words, the nature of autobiographical memory mediates the account (see also Rosen 1998). This may well lead to inconsistencies and contradictions in the narrative, and the process is likely on the whole to be self-serving in character. Moreover, even though they are written after the event, they may be just as self-deceiving as diaries and letters. These problems justify a good deal of caution in using autobiographies as sources. Nevertheless, they remain useful when analysed in the light of such issues. No less than with diaries and letters, their biases, inconsistencies and even their self-deceit make them fascinating quarries of evidence about the nature of individual lives. They are 'true to life', in Crossman's phrase, because of these traits and not despite them.

Even though they may be absorbed in the telling of their author's own life story, autobiographies also offer interesting insights into broader social and public dimensions. This is a point of contention for some commentators. For example, Pascal (1960) claimed that a distinction should be made between an autobiography, which was focused principally on the self, and the memoir or reminiscence, which was mainly about encounters with others. However, such a definition is in practice difficult to reconcile with the overlapping and complex nature of the 'private' and 'public' domains. An important characteristic of autobiographies, as with diaries and letters, is that, although they are recognised above all as personal documents, they shed light not only on their life but also on their times. They reflect interconnections with other lives, within the same family and often far beyond, and in different contexts over the course of the lifetime (*Sociology* 1993, p. 2). Moreover, they can give rich insights into social relationships more generally. As Mary Evans has suggested, 'a study of the individual illustrates the social, and re-affirms the centrality of certain general themes in the lives of all particular individuals' (Evans 1993, p. 8). Conversely, the accounts of politicians and other leading figures may emphasise their involvement in great public events, but will also be concerned to relate these to their own personal, individual development.

The autobiographies left by ordinary people demonstrate the inter-connections between the record of the individual life and the family and wider social group. David Vincent's major study of working-class auto-biographies of nineteenth-century England, based on 142 published and unpublished works of this type, shows that such authors were highly con-scious of their involvement in a network of family, friends, colleagues and acquaintances. Their reminiscences of education emphasise the overriding importance of the family economy (Vincent 1981, p. 94). Their writing about their adult lives attempts to connect the public side of their person-alities with their private emotional experiences (Vincent 1981, p. 39). It is important to appreciate that in dealing with their private and home life they tend to draw a discreet veil over areas that they feel it improper or unnecessary to discuss, and especially about taboo subjects (Vincent 1981, p. 41). So far as their approach to the outside world is concerned, Vincent finds a very wide range of attitudes: 'No two men displayed the same pattern of responses, but equally none followed a straight, untroubled path towards the goal of self-improvement' (Vincent 1981, p. 184; see also Burnett 1974, 1982). Women tended to be confined to domestic roles, a position generally reflected in the domestic memoirs that they produced, but still, as Linda Peterson attests, these memoirs preserve invaluable information about atti-tudes, customs and conditions of the time, and represent in their own right 'important documents of cultural history, evidence testifying to the flourish-ing Victorian cult of domesticity' (Peterson 1999, p. 21).

The autobiographies of public figures often reveal many details of the personal and private backgrounds, as well as of their involvement in the public and political scene. The British Labour Party politician Roy Hattersley, for example, has written both a moving memoir of his Yorkshire boyhood in the 1930s and 1940s (Hattersley 1990), and reminiscences with what he calls 'scenes from a political life'. His memories of his youth are filled with vivid, and sometimes, as he concedes, 'retrospectively painted' (p. 11), recall of relationships and situations, as in the following:

> So we rented 174 Wadsley Lane, a large, dilapidated, late Victorian villa in a continuous – though irregular – terrace that ran up one of the steeply sloping roads which give Sheffield suburbs their distinctive

character. We left Wadsley Road when I was six, but by the time that we moved to the superior security of owner-occupation I had developed a clear perception of the social hierarchy within our little group of families. On one side of us lived the Moores, a large family which included an elder son with ambition to become a dance band drummer. He practised assiduously late at night in his bedroom. They lived higher up the hill, but lower down some imaginary league table. Nobody doubted that our arrival had improved the tone of the neighbourhood. The previous tenants of 174 had, we were told, gone to *The Horse and Jockey* every night, leaving their children to amuse themselves with hammers and nails. When we moved in, the skirting boards and the door jambs were riddled with holes as if they had been ravaged by giant woodworm.

(Hattersley 1990, p. 13)

Quite apart from the extraordinary detail of this account, it gives the infant Hattersley credit for insight and observation well beyond his years, and might well owe something to the imagination. This work is interesting also for the connections that it develops between the author's own development and his generation's experience of what he describes as the social revolution of the 1940s. As he explains, '*A Yorkshire Boyhood* was meant to be the story of the generation which was born during the great depression, brought up in the war and propelled through adolescence by the gentle revolution which began in 1945. I was simply an example of life in those extraordinary times' (Hattersley 1990, p. xiii). Thus, while focusing on himself and his family, it has broader social and indeed political implications that are intended to help explain his later career.

Hattersley's political memoir, while dominated by the infighting of government and opposition, also gives intriguing glimpses of the relationship between the 'public' and the 'private', for example in his recollection of the death of one of his political heroes, Hugh Gaitskell, when leader of the Labour Party:

Hugh Gaitskell died in January 1963. His death was announced on the Friday evening and, on a Saturday morning now clouded in my mind with the memory of grief, two events stand out in the gloom. A neighbour, Anita Hirston by name, stopped me on the road to say that her ideological objection to joining the Labour Party has been removed and that she would be grateful for my advice about where to obtain a membership application form. Instead of abusing her as she deserved, I burst into tears. And it should have been a day of joy. For there flopped through my letter box a long buff envelope, postmarked Birmingham 11, containing one of the bright yellow forms which had become well known to me. The Fox Hollies ward of the Sparkbrook

Constituency Labour Party had nominated me for consideration as prospective parliamentary candidate.

(Hattersley 1996, p. 35)

It may be that this recollection is also 'retrospectively painted', but none the less it evokes humanity and private pain in the midst of the larger rhythms of national politics.

It is interesting too that, in many of the political autobiographies that have burgeoned in recent years, discussions of the personal and private background and of family and schooling are not merely an accessory but occupy a central role in the account as a whole. That is, the author's construction of the personal becomes a key explanatory device designed to demonstrate why they approach the public arena in the way that they do, and why they take up particular positions on specific social and political issues. For example, the memoirs of the former British Prime Minister Margaret Thatcher recall the reasons for her delight at being made education spokesperson for the Conservative party in the late 1960s:

I knew that I had risen to my present position as a result of free (or nearly free) good education, and I wanted others to have the same chance. Socialist education policies, by equalising downwards and denying gifted children the opportunity to get on, were a major obstacle to that. I was also fascinated by the scientific side – the portfolio in those days being to shadow the Department of Education *and* Science. Moreover, I suspect that women, or at least mothers, have an instinctive interest in the education of children.

(Thatcher 1995, pp. 156–7)

In this passage, then, Thatcher is enlisting her own education, her training as a scientist and her position as a woman and a mother as credentials for her upward political progress. There is no space at all between the 'personal' and the 'public', in fact they are intertwined. Even more significantly, Thatcher goes on to develop a general theory of attitudes towards State education on the part of British Conservatives that is based entirely on where they themselves went to school, or their own personal involvement in education. She suggested that there were four different attitudes current among Conservatives:

First, there were those who had no real interest in state education in any case because they themselves and their children went to private schools. This was an important group, all too likely to be swayed by arguments of political expediency. Second, there were those who, themselves or their children, had failed to get into grammar school and had been disappointed with the education received at a secondary modern.

Third, there were those Conservatives who, either because they themselves were teachers or through some other contact with the world of
education, had absorbed a large dose of the fashionable egalitarian doctrines of the day. Finally, there were people like me who had been to
good grammar schools, were strongly opposed to their destruction and
felt no inhibitions at all about arguing for the 11-Plus [examination].

(Thatcher 1995, p. 157)

Her vision of 'people like me', drawing on her personal memories of childhood, education and family, here seems connected to her ideas about people
who were 'one of us', defined by Hugo Young as 'the politicians and other
advisers on whom she felt she could rely' (Young 1991, p. ix).

It is also useful to compare her own account with those of others who
have written at length on her political career. Young's work, published
before Thatcher's memoirs, points out that she represented a very different
approach from that of her predecessor as shadow education spokesperson,
Edward Boyle, who was more sympathetic to the development of comprehensive schools (Young 1991, pp. 66–7). Boyle had been educated at a
public school, and so Thatcher's categorisation of Conservative attitudes
may well be in part a code to dismiss his approach as being 'swayed by
arguments of political expediency'. Thatcher's later biographer, John
Campbell, also notes the differences between Boyle and Thatcher:

A gentle, liberal, high-minded Old Etonian baronet who had already
been Education Secretary in 1962–4, Boyle personified the educational
consensus which had promoted comprehensive schools and 'progressive' teaching methods . . . Angry Conservatives in the shires and
suburbs fighting to preserve their grammar schools regarded Boyle as
a traitor – a socialist in all but name. Mrs Thatcher – grammar-
school-educated, defiantly middle-class and strenuously anti-socialist –
was in every way his opposite.

(Campbell 2001, pp. 192–3)

On the other hand, Thatcher had been educated at the University of Oxford
at the same time as Boyle, and also sent her own children to public schools.
The point here is that Thatcher's political autobiography, with its assertions
and rationalisations, needs to be treated carefully as a documentary source
and tested against other accounts.

Another political autobiography, that of another former British Prime
Minister, James Callaghan, raises similar issues but is also a means of
assessing the diary accounts of members of his own Cabinet such as Tony
Benn. Callaghan's account also emphasises the personal in explaining his
interest in education, and more particularly his decision to open the 'Great
Debate' of 1976:

> I have always been a convinced believer in the importance of education, as throughout my life I had seen how many doors it could unlock for working-class children who had begun with few other advantages, and I regretted my own lack of a university education. I was also aware of growing concerns among parents about the direction some schools were taking and I was anxious to probe this.
>
> (Callaghan 1987, p. 409)

He explains the purposes underpinning his Ruskin College speech in the following terms:

> My general guidance for the speech was that it should begin a debate about existing educational trends and should ask some controversial questions. It should avoid blandness and bring out the criticisms I had heard, whilst explaining the value of the teachers' work and the need for parents to be closely associated with their children's schools. It should ask why industry's status was so low in young people's choice of careers, and the reasons for the shortage of mathematics and science teachers.
>
> (Callaghan 1987, p. 410)

However, as he recalls it, at this stage his mission was made more difficult as he 'tripped over some appalling educational snobbery'. The *Times Educational Supplement*, using a memorandum from the Secretary of State for education to the Prime Minister, wrote an article that was 'both scornful and cynical about my intention'. This then led to 'a chain reaction in other newspapers and the chalk-dust flew'. The Conservative opposition and the National Union of Teachers began to voice criticisms: 'It was obvious that there was much suppressed questioning which had only needed an accidental trigger to set it off. Part of my aim was already achieved, and the Great Debate I had hoped to launch had left the slipway and entered the water even before I had time to crash the bottle of champagne on its bows.' A student demonstration then met him when he delivered his speech at Ruskin College (Callaghan 1987, p. 410).

Callaghan's recollections of this event helpfully illustrate some of the general problems of autobiographical accounts. It is above all else self-justifying as it seeks to explain his reasons for intervening in an unprecedented way in this contentious area of social policy. It also owes much to the wisdom of hindsight as he traces the factors involved and the public debate that would intensify further over the following decade. Moreover, it is also significant for what it omits, as he stresses the opposition encountered as reaction from the media, but does not mention the arguments raised within his own party and even within his own Cabinet. The diary account of Tony Benn (Case Study 6, above) makes it clear that there was impassioned opposition to these developments, at least from Benn himself. On the other hand, Benn's diary entry of 25 October endorses Callaghan's account of the reasons advanced for this initiative. How far Shirley Williams was herself involved in these early discussions around the 'Great Debate' is left unclear in Callaghan's account. It will require other sources, including perhaps her own story and also the relevant papers of the Department of Education and Science when these become publicly available, to clarify this and other remaining issues. Other important sources for future researchers will include Benn's full unpublished diary, which should be scrutinised with due care, and also hopefully Callaghan's personal papers.

Overall, as has been seen throughout this chapter, diaries, letters and autobiographies are highly valuable documentary sources for historians and social researchers. They offer different things but also have much in common with each other for the insights they offer. They give important and often unique insights into the detail and variety of life as viewed by individuals, 'true to life' even in their most problematic characteristics. They are also significant evidence on the times we live in. Their value may also be gauged, perhaps most profoundly, from the way that they can relate the different domains of modern societies, and to document both our life and our times.

Suggestions for further reading

Benn, T. (1990) *Against the Tide: Diaries 1973–76*, edited by Ruth Winstone, Arrow, London

Callaghan, J. (1987) *Time and Chance*, Collins, London

Crossman, R. (1975) *The Diaries of a Cabinet Minister*, vol. 1: *Minister of Housing 1964–66*, Hamish Hamilton and Jonathan Cape, London

Earle, R. (ed.) (1999) *Epistolary Selves: Letters and Letter-Writers, 1600–1945*, Ashgate, Aldershot

Heward, C. (1988) *Making a Man of Him: Parents and Their Sons' Education at an English Public School, 1929–50*, Routledge, London

Ponsonby, A. (1923) *English Diaries: A Review of English Diaries from the Sixteenth to the Twentieth Century with an Introduction on Diary Writing*, Methuen, London

Sociology (1993) special issue, Biography and autobiography in sociology, 27/1

Vincent, J. (1981) *Bread, Knowledge and Freedom: A Study of Nineteenth-Century Working Class Autobiography*, Methuen, London

7   A New Leaf

Connections and Conclusions

This book has argued that there is an important role to be found for documentary studies in education, history and the social sciences. For historians, this in itself on one level merely confirms the dominant practices of the historical profession for the past two centuries. Yet it is salutary also to articulate and to externalise these usages, rather than to leave them internalised, implicit and undertheorised. My intention has been also to help to draw out connections between historians and social scientists, both actual and potential, in the research uses found for the documents around us. If history is to be the 'shank of social study', as C. Wright Mills (1959) envisaged, this process of drawing out connections still has far to run, but it is a project that is worthy of engaging the attention of historians in the future.

For educators and social researchers, the task of this book has been different. It has been to revive the awareness of documents that was so strong in the early twentieth century. More than this, it has also been to try to assert a place for documentary studies for researchers of the twenty-first century. Here too there are connections to be made, especially to enhance appreciation for the historical dimension of education and society. This should be advanced through a renewed understanding of the continuities and changes of print culture in all its many forms, no less than in a consciousness of the profusion of documentary evidence in the world of today.

As well as exploring the interface of past and present, I have also pursued the tensions and interactions between the public and the private in the development of documentary studies. It has been evident throughout that, while public and private are powerful constructs that represent separate and distinct domains, documentary study can shed light on how they influence and act on each other in practice. National archives can take us into intimate, personal, everyday concerns; a private diary can illuminate the affairs of state. A rigid typology of 'personal documents' and 'public records' is therefore unsatisfactory and inadequate for our purposes.

We have found a very wide range of documentary sources, each with their own problems and potential uses for researchers: primary, secondary, solicited, unsolicited, paper-based, virtual, archival records, books, newspapers, periodicals, works of fiction, official data and proceedings, reports, diaries, letters and autobiographies. Each of these constitute substantial and significant sets of documents in their own right, and documentary researchers may well wish to concentrate their efforts on a particular type. However, there are also connections to be made in relating different kinds of documentary sources to each other. This may be viewed in terms of triangulation, defined as the combination of methods or sources of data in a single study (Taylor and Bogdan 1998, p. 80). As Taylor and Bogdan remark, triangulation may be useful as a means of checking insights drawn from different sources of data, and in order to gain a deeper and clearer understanding of the situation and the people involved (Taylor and Bogdan 1998, p. 80).

Although documentary research is often thought of as one single type of source, it actually offers a number of different perspectives from which to view a given problem or topic. We have already come across several of these in the preceding chapters. For example, the combination of a published report and the archival records of the committee that produced it will give more insight into the nature of the report than either of them on their own. Similarly, comparing the letters sent by a particular person with the diary kept by that person over the same period will give a fuller picture than would be possible by using just one of these sources. The differing perspectives of the protagonists involved in a particular incident, whether individuals or organisations, can also be gleaned by employing a range of documentary sources rather than just one type. There is an important sense therefore in which methodological pluralism can be attained through the use of different types of documentary sources.

A broader notion of triangulation and methodological pluralism is possible also through a combination of documentary and non-documentary sources. Probably the most common approach to developing such a combination is to relate archival records to interviews of living respondents. A useful example of this kind of approach is discussed by Saran (1985), who applies it to the development of education policy since 1945. Such research is often conceived as interdisciplinary in that the archival documentary sources involve 'historical' skills, while interviews are the natural domain of 'sociological' insights. Thus, there remains a theoretical division of labour in this kind of research project that goes to the heart of underlying tensions between past and present, history and the social sciences, but once again this familiar dichotomy can be challenged and even transcended.

A recent example of this form of methodological pluralism is reported on by Karen Duke (2002). Duke examines the role and influence of policy networks in the development of prison drugs policy, and the associated research problems of access, knowledge and power. She uses a case study based upon a strategy of methodological triangulation involving documentary analysis and semi-structured interviews. The documents used were mainly published State sources, including documents relating to prison drugs policy, penal and criminal justice policy, national drugs policy and Advisory Council on the Misuse of Drugs reports, together with annual reports and other documentation provided by penal reform groups, drug agencies and professional associations. Interviews were then conducted with those involved in policy networks to find out more about their perceptions and experiences of drugs as an issue, the policies and the processes involved in their development. According to Duke, these methods were interconnected, 'with the documentary analysis informing the direction and focus of the interviews and providing historical and contextual data, while the interviews influenced further analyses and explorations of the documents' (Duke 2002, p. 43).

One instance of methodological pluralism in which I have been involved is a project on teacher professionalism in England and the effects of the National Curriculum and associated policy changes since the Education Reform Act of 1988. This was approached in two complementary ways. First, documentary sources were examined to assess changes in the idea of teacher professionalism over the past fifty years. Archival records were analysed in depth, especially those of the Ministry of Education and the Department of Education and Science at the Public Record Office in London for the 1950s and 1960s, but also institutional and personal archives. A number of publicly available documents were also assessed, including reports and newspapers over this period. Secondly, teachers and policy makers were interviewed to find out their experiences and understandings of teacher professionalism. These complementary strategies allowed an enhanced understanding of changes and continuities over time, especially of older forms of teacher professionalism and their supplanting through the challenges of the 1990s (see McCulloch, Helsby and Knight 2000). There was in this to some extent a demarcation between the historical and the contemporary, that is, between an appraisal of the so-called 'secret garden' of teachers in the 1950s and 1960s, and an understanding of the effects of greater accountability and state control since the 1980s. Nevertheless, there was an important interactive element in the project. For example, the teachers and policy makers who were interviewed were asked about their memories of teacher professionalism before 1988. Some of them could remember this at first hand, while others could report on what they had been told by others. These memories could then be compared and contrasted with the contemporary accounts provided by documentary sources of the 1960s, 1970s and 1980s. This generated interesting insights into the nature of social memory among teachers and policy makers, while also providing grounds for a careful reconstruction of changes over time (McCulloch, Helsby and Knight 2000, especially chapter 4).

Another very interesting case is the project on Kensington Elementary School in the United States conducted by Louis Smith and colleagues, based on a combination or 'blending' in their terms of historical and ethnographic method. In this study they emphasise that triangulation and multimethods, which they value highly in their approach to ethnographic research, reappear in their developing perspective on historical method (Smith *et al.* 1988, p. 25). In exploring the changes at the school since its opening in the 1960s, they began to study the minutes of the local School Board. This led in turn to two years of intensive reading of these minutes from 1915 to the present, together with interviews with a wide range of former students and older members of the community. Their account of how this project broadened in this way reflects the 'energizing' and 'creative' nature of the process, in what they describe as 'an incredibly important all-encompassing professional experience' (Smith *et al.* 1988, p. 30). Moreover, lines of demarcation between history and ethnography appeared to merge into 'a general open-ended set of field methods' (Smith *et al.* 1988, p. 37). They also note examples of triangulation that in their view blended document analysis with brief interviews. Indeed, they insist,

> We found an easy flow back and forth between the kinds of data that we looked for and generated. Documents and interviews and observations seemed to demand many of the same skills and perceptiveness as their adequacy was challenged and as sense was to be made of them. Important modes of checking validity of information, such as triangulation, seemed equally appropriate within and across historical and ethnographic data. The historians' concept of primary sources enabled us to perceive the work of the participant observer in a fresh light.
>
> (Smith *et al.* 1988, p. 41)

This is therefore a fascinating example of pluralist methodology in which methods are not simply combined, nor even merely interactive, but actually blend to enhance an understanding of a specific case.

This seems an appropriate note on which to conclude the present work, which has emphasised throughout the importance of documentary study for research in education, history and the social sciences. Documents are often neglected and taken for granted, estranged and alienated even in their familiarity, propinquity and abundance. Nevertheless, they form a basis for a renewed understanding of our social and historical world. Perhaps, also, documentary studies may encourage mutual understanding and regard across the disciplinary barriers, and a fresh awareness of the research challenges that we have in common. This would indeed be to turn over a new leaf, the oldest documentary method of all. What will we find on the next page?

Suggestions for further reading

McCulloch, G., Helsby, G., Knight, P. (2000) *The Politics of Professionalism: Teachers and the Curriculum*, Continuum, London

Saran, R. (1985) The use of archives and interviews in research on education policy. In R. Burgess (ed.), *Strategies of Educational Research: Qualitative Methods*, Falmer, London, pp. 207–41

Smith, L.M., Dwyer, D.C., Prunty, J.J., Kleine, P.F. (1988) *Innovation and Change in Schooling: History, Politics, and Agency*, Falmer, London

Bibliography

Archival sources

Association of Education Committees papers, University of Leeds Special Collections, file A511, on Curriculum Study Group, 1962:
    Dame Mary Smieton to Sir William Alexander, 9 March 1962
    Sir William Alexander to Dame Mary Smieton, 11 March 1962
Bristol Grammar School papers, Bristol records office:
    BGS board of governors meeting, 9 November 1911, minute book 3
Laski, H., Hull University Library:
    C. Attlee to H. Laski, 20 August 1945 (file 13)
Ministry of Education, Public Record Office, London:
    Wood, Sir R., minute, 15 April 1946, ED.136/787
    Newsom committee papers, 1962–63, ED.146/45, ED.146/46
New Zealand Department of Education papers, Auckland, New Zealand (Northern Regional Office)
    26/1/88, 26/1/89: minutes of investigating committee, correspondence, reports and memoranda on juvenile gangs in Auckland, New Zealand, 1970
New Zealand Department of Education papers, Wellington, New Zealand
    34/1/3/1 Part 9: Secondary education – general – secondary schools enrolment schemes, correspondence between parents and Minister of Education, 1984
Norwood, C., University of Sheffield Special Collections:
    Cyril Norwood to Catherine Kilner, 17 November 1901
    Cyril and Catherine Norwood, handwritten notes, n.d. [1933]
Raybould, S., University of Leeds Special Collections:
    Crowther committee papers, 1956–59 (Box 10)
Trades Union Congress, Modern Records Centre, University of Warwick (Mss 292)
Wales High School, Rotherham:
    Technical and Vocational Education Initiative Inset Day, 7 March 1989 (file 73)
Wolverhampton Technical High School log book, Pendeford High School

Websites

http://www.archives.gov.nz – Archives New Zealand
http://www.census.ac.uk – online census data, UK

Bibliography

http://www.data-archive.ac.uk – UK Data Archive including data of National Child Development Study, UK

http://www.dfes.gov.uk – Department for Education and Skills, UK

http://www.dfes.gov.uk/statistics – DfES statistics including data for Youth Cohort Study of England and Wales

http://www.economist.co.uk – *The Economist* weekly periodical, UK

http://www.education.guardian.co.uk/ – Education Guardian weekly supplement to *The Guardian* newspaper, UK

http://www.gpoaccess.gov/crecord/index.html – Congressional Record, USA

http://www.guardian.co.uk – *The Guardian* newspaper, UK

http://www.hmso.gov.uk – legislation, government information, official publications, UK

http://www.hmso.gov.uk/acts/acts1998/19980029.htm – Data Protection Act (1998), UK

http://www.hmso.gov.uk/acts/acts2000/20000036.htm – Freedom of Information Act (2000), UK

http://www.mimas.ac.uk/macro_econ/ – International Data Service

http://www.mirror.co.uk/news – *The Daily Mirror* newspaper, UK

http://modernrecords.warwick.ac.uk/sumguide.shtml – Modern Records Centre catalogue, University of Warwick, UK

http://www.movinghere.org.uk – History of Migration website, UK

http://www.nationalarchives.gov.uk – National Archives, UK

http://www.newstatesman.co.uk – *The New Statesman* weekly periodical, UK

http://www.parliament.uk – Bills, committee proceedings, parliamentary publications, register of interests etc., UK

http://www.parliament.the-stationery-office.co.uk – Hansard, UK

http://www.pro.gov.uk – Public Record Office, UK

http://www.pro.gov.uk/census/ – online census site, 1901 census, UK

http://www.pro-online.pro.gov.uk – Public Record Office online catalogue, UK
CAB 128/50/55 – minutes of British Cabinet meeting, 30 November 1972

http://www.spectator.co.uk – *The Spectator* weekly periodical, UK

http://www.statistics.gov.uk – official government statistics including annual Social Trends, UK

http://www.swarb.co.uk/acts/1988CopyrightDesignsandPatents01Act.html – Copyright, Designs and Patents Act (1988), UK

http://www.tes.co.uk – *Times Educational Supplement* weekly periodical, UK

http://www.thes.co.uk – *Times Higher Education Supplement* weekly periodical, UK

Books and articles

All quotations are from the last edition cited unless otherwise stated.

AHIER, J. (1988) *Industry, Children and the Nation: An Analysis of National Identity in School Textbooks*, Falmer, London

ALLPORT, G.W. (1947) *The Use of Personal Documents in Psychological Science*, Social Science Research Council, New York

ANDREW, A. (1985) In pursuit of the past: some problems in the collection, analysis and use of historical documentary evidence. In R. Burgess (ed.), *Strategies of Educational Research: Qualitative Methods*, Falmer, London, pp. 153–78

ANGELL, R. (1947) A critical review of the development of the personal document method in sociology, 1920–1940, in L. Gottschalk, C. Kluckhohn and R. Angell, *The Use of Personal Documents in History, Anthropology, and Sociology*, Social Science Research Council, New York, pp. 175–232

APPLE, M., CHRISTIAN-SMITH, L. (1991) The politics of the textbook. In M. Apple, L. Christian-Smith (eds), *The Politics of the Textbook*, Routledge, London, pp. 1–21

AUCKLAND METRO (1984) The Auckland Grammar mystique, May, 35, pp. 36–54

AUCKLAND METRO (1986) Three months in another town, October, 64, pp. 172–84

AUCKLAND STAR (1989) report, Pupil migration: which schools attract most out-of-zone pupils, which lose most, 30 May

BALL, S. (1990) *Politics and Policy Making in Education: Explorations in Policy Sociology*, Routledge, London

BARTHES, R. (1977) The death of the author. In R. Barthes, *Image, Music, Text*, Fontana, London, pp. 142–8

BENN, T. (1990) *Against the Tide: Diaries 1973–76*, edited by Ruth Winstone, Arrow, London

BENN, T. (1995) *Years of Hope: Diaries, Papers and Letters, 1940–1962*, edited by Ruth Winstone, Arrow, London

BENN, T. (2002) *Free at Last! Diaries 1991–2001*, edited by Ruth Winstone, Arrow, London

BERGER, M. (1977) *Real and Imagined Worlds: The Novel and Social Science*, Harvard University Press, London

BEVAN, A. (2002) *Tracing Your Ancestors at the Public Record Office*, 6th edn, Public Record Office, London

BEVERIDGE, W. (1942) *Social Insurance and Allied Services* (Beveridge Report), Cmd 6404, HMSO, London

BLISHEN, E. (1955) *Roaring Boys: A Schoolmaster's Agony*, Thames and Hudson, London

BLODGETT, H. (1988) *Centuries of Female Days: Englishwomen's Private Diaries*, Rutgers University Press, New Brunswick, NJ

BLUMER, H. (1939) *An Appraisal of Thomas and Znaniecki's* The Polish Peasant in Europe and America, Critiques of Research in the Social Sciences, I; Social Science Research Council, New York

BOARD OF EDUCATION (1938) *Secondary Education with Special Reference to Grammar Schools and Technical High Schools* (Spens Report), HMSO, London

BOARD OF EDUCATION (1943a) *Curriculum and Examinations in Secondary Schools* (Norwood Report), HMSO, London

BOARD OF EDUCATION (1943b) *Educational Reconstruction*, Cmd 6458, HMSO, London

BOARD OF EDUCATION (1944) *The Public Schools and the General Educational System* (Fleming Report), HMSO, London

BOWE, R. and BALL, S., with GOLD, A. (1992) *Reforming Education and Changing Schools: Case Studies in Policy Sociology*, Routledge, London

Bibliography

BRIGGS, A., BURKE, P. (2002) *A Social History of the Media: From Gutenberg to the Internet*, Polity, Cambridge

BURGESS, R. (1984a) *In the Field: An Introduction to Field Research*, Routledge, London

BURGESS, R. (ed.) (1984b) *The Research Process in Educational Settings: Ten Case Studies*, Falmer, London

BURGESS, R. (ed.) (1985) *Strategies of Educational Research: Qualitative Methods*, Falmer, London

BURKE, S. (1992) *The Death and Return of the Author: Criticism and Subjectivity in Barthes, Foucault and Derrida*, Edinburgh University Press, Edinburgh

BURNETT, J. (1974) Preface: autobiographies as history. In J. Burnett (ed.) *Useful Toil: Autobiographies of Working People from the 1820s to the 1920s*, Allen Lane, London, pp. 1–19

BURNETT, J. (1982) Preface: Autobiographies as history. In J. Burnett (ed.), *Destiny Obscure: Autobiographies of Childhood, Education and the Family from the 1820s to the 1920s*, Allen Lane, London, pp. 1–17

BURTON, D. (ed.) (2000a) *Research Training for Social Scientists: A Handbook for Postgraduate Researchers*, Sage, London

BURTON, D. (2000b) Secondary data analysis. In D. Burton (ed.), *Research Training for Social Scientists*, Sage, London, pp. 347–62

CADOGAN, M., CRAIG, P. (1986) *You're a Brick, Angela! The Girls' Story 1839–1985*, Gollancz, London

CALHOUN, C. (ed.) (1992) *Habermas and the Public Sphere*, MIT Press, London

CALLAGHAN, J. (1987) *Time and Chance*, Collins, London

CAMPBELL, J. (2001) *Margaret Thatcher*, vol. 1: *The Grocer's Daughter*, Pimlico, London

CANTWELL, J.D. (1991) *The Public Record Office 1838–1958*, HMSO, London

CARTER, I. (1990) *Ancient Cultures of Conceit: British University Fiction in the Post-War Years*, Routledge, London

CHARTIER, R. (1987) *The Cultural Uses of Print in Early Modern Europe*, Princeton University Press, Princeton, NJ

CHARTIER, R. (1988) General introduction: print culture. In R. Chartier (ed.), *The Culture of Print: Power and the Use of Print in Early Modern Europe*, Princeton University Press, Princeton, NJ, pp. 1–10

CLARK, A. (1994) *Diaries*, Phoenix, London

CLARK, A. (2001) *Diaries: Into Politics*, edited by Ion Trewin, Phoenix, London

CLARKE, F. (1940) *Education and Social Change: An English Interpretation*, Sheldon Press, London

CLARKE, P. (1996) *Hope and Glory: Britain 1900–1990*, Penguin Books, London

CODD, J. (1988) The construction and deconstruction of educational policy documents, *Journal of Education Policy*, 3/3, pp. 235–47

COHEN, S. (1999) *Challenging Orthodoxies: Toward a New Cultural History of Education*, Peter Lang, New York

COLLEY, L. (1989) *Namier*, Weidenfeld and Nicolson, London

COLLINS, P. (1963) *Dickens and Education*, Macmillan, London

CONNOR, S. (1996) *The English Novel in History, 1950–1995*, Routledge, London

COSER, L.A. (1979) American trends, in T. Bottomore, R. Nisbet (eds), *A History of Sociological Analysis*, Heinemann, London, pp. 287–320

COWLING, M. (1971) *The Impact of Labour 1920–1924*, Cambridge University Press, Cambridge

COX, N. (1990) The thirty-year rule and freedom of information: access to Government records. In G.H. Martin, P. Spufford (eds), *The Records of the Nation*, Boydell Press/British Record Society, London, pp. 75–86

CROSSMAN, R. (1975) *The Diaries of a Cabinet Minister*, vol. 1: *Minister of Housing 1964–66*, Hamish Hamilton and Jonathan Cape, London

CROSSMAN, R. (1981) *The Backbench Diaries of Richard Crossman*, edited by Janet Morgan, Hamish Hamilton, London

CUNNINGHAM, P. (1992) Teachers' professional image and the Press 1950–1990, *History of Education*, 21/1, pp. 37–56

CURRIE, E. (2002) *Diaries*, Time Warner, London

DALTON, H. (1953) *Call Back Yesterday: Memoirs 1887–1931*, Frederick Muller, London

DALTON, H. (1957) *The Fateful Years: Memoirs 1931–1945*, Frederick Muller, London

DALTON, H. (1962) *High Tide and After: Memoirs 1945–1960*, Frederick Muller, London

DEARING, R. (1996) *Review of Qualifications for 16–19 Year Olds: Full Report*, School Curriculum and Assessment Authority, London

DEPARTMENT FOR EDUCATION (1992) *Choice and Diversity*, HMSO, London

DEPARTMENT FOR EDUCATION AND EMPLOYMENT (1997) *Excellence in Schools*, Stationery Office, London

DEPARTMENT FOR EDUCATION AND SKILLS (2003) *The Future of Higher Education*, Cm 5735, Stationery Office, London

DEPARTMENT OF EDUCATION AND SCIENCE (1967) *Children and Their Primary Schools* (Plowden Report), HMSO, London

DERRIDA, J. (1995) Archive fever: a Freudian impression, *Diacritics*, 25/2, pp. 9–63

DUKE, K. (2002) Getting beyond the 'official line': reflections on dilemmas of access, knowledge and power in researching policy networks, *Journal of Social Policy*, 31/1, pp. 39–59

DURKHEIM, E. (1927/1950) *The Rules of Sociological Method*, 8th edition, Free Press, New York

DURKHEIM, E. (1938/1977) *The Evolution of Educational Thought: Lectures on the Formation and Development of Secondary Education in France*, Routledge and Kegan Paul, London

DURKHEIM, E. (1951) *Suicide*, Free Press, New York

EARLE, R. (1999) Introduction: letters, writers and the historian. In R. Earle (ed.), *Epistolary Selves: Letters and Letter-Writers, 1600–1945*, Ashgate, Aldershot, pp. 1–12

ELEY, G. (1992) Nations, publics, and political cultures: placing Habermas in the nineteenth century. In C. Calhoun (ed.), *Habermas and the Public Sphere*, MIT Press, London, pp. 289–339

ENCYCLOPAEDIA BRITANNICA (1974) 15th edn, vol. 1, Micropaedia, 'Archives', pp. 530–31, University of Chicago Press, Chicago

Bibliography

EVANS, M. (1993) Reading lives: how the personal might be social, *Sociology*, 27/1, pp. 5–13

EVANS, R. (1997) *In Defence of History*, Granta Books, London

FAIRCLOUGH, N. (1995) *Critical Discourse Analysis: The Critical Study of Language*, Longman, London

FEBVRE, L., Martin, H.-J. (1958/1984) *The Coming of the Book: The Impact of Printing*, Verso, London

FINCH, J. (1986) *Research and Policy: The Uses of Qualitative Methods in Social and Educational Research*, Falmer, London

FOSTER, S. (1999) The struggle for American identity: treatment of ethnic groups in United States history textbooks, *History of Education*, 28/3, pp. 251–78

FOTHERGILL, R.A. (1974) *Private Chronicles: A Study of English Diaries*, Oxford University Press, London

FOX, P. (1994) *Shame and Resistance in the British Working-Class Novel, 1890–1945*, Duke University Press, London

GARFINKEL, H. (1967) *Studies in Ethnomethodology*, Prentice-Hall, Englewood Cliffs, NJ

GAY, P. (1970) *The Enlightenment: An Interpretation*, vol. 2: *The Science of Freedom*, Weidenfeld and Nicolson, London

GILES, G.C.T. (1946) *The New School Tie*, Pilot Press, London

GOODSON, I. (1985) History, context and qualitative methods in the study of curriculum. In R. Burgess (ed.), *Strategies of Educational Research: Qualitative Methods*, Falmer, London, pp. 121–51

GOODSON, I., SIKES, P. (2001) *Life History Research in Educational Settings: Learning from Lives*, Open University Press, Buckingham

GORARD, S. (2001) *Quantitative Methods in Educational Research: The Role of Numbers Made Easy*, Continuum, London

GORARD, S. (2002) The role of secondary data in combining methodological approaches, *Educational Review*, 54/3, pp. 231–7

GOSDEN, P. (1981) Twentieth-century archives of education as sources for the study of education policy and administration, *Archives*, 66, pp. 86–95

GOTTSCHALK, L., KLUCKHOHN, C., ANGELL, R. (1947) *The Use of Personal Documents in History, Anthropology, and Sociology*, Social Science Research Council, New York

GUARDIAN, THE (2002) Edwardian census chokes the Internet, 3 January, p. 17

GUARDIAN, THE (2003a) Memories caught on the brink of extinction, 3 January, p. 17

GUARDIAN, THE (2003b) Online archive brings Britain's migration story to life, 30 July, p. 7

HABERMAS, J. (1992) *The Structural Transformation of the Public Sphere: An Inquiry into a Category of Bourgeois Society*, Polity, London

HAKIM, C. (1980) Census reports as documentary evidence: the census commentaries 1801–1951, *Sociological Review*, 28/3, pp. 551–80

HAKIM, C. (1982) *Secondary Analysis in Social Research: A Guide to Data Sources and Methods with Examples*, George Allen and Unwin, London

HALL, L.A. (1991) *Hidden Anxieties: Male Sexuality, 1900–1950*, Polity, Cambridge

HALSEY, A.H., FLOUD, J., ANDERSON, C.A. (eds) (1961) *Education, Economy and Society*, Free Press, New York

HALSEY, A.H., HEATH, A.F., RIDGE, J.M. (1980) *Origins and Destinations: Family, Class and Education in Modern Britain*, Clarendon, Oxford

HALSTEAD, M. (1988) *Education, Justice and Cultural Diversity: An Examination of the Honeyford Affair, 1984–85*, Falmer, London

HARBER, C. (1997) Using documents for qualitative educational research in Africa. In M. Crossley, G. Vulliamy (eds), *Qualitative Educational Research in Developing Countries: Current Perspectives*, Garland, London, pp. 113–31

HARTLEY, J. (1999) Letters are *everything* these days: mothers and letters in the Second World War. In R. Earle (ed.), *Epistolary Selves*, Aldgate, Aldershot, pp. 183–95

HATTERSLEY, R. (1990) *My Yorkshire Boyhood*, Pan, London

HATTERSLEY, R. (1996) *Who Goes Home?: Scenes from a Political Life*, Warner, London

HELSBY, G., McCULLOCH, G. (eds) (1997) *Teachers and the National Curriculum*, Cassell, London

HEWARD, C. (1988) *Making a Man of Him: Parents and Their Sons' Education at an English Public School, 1929–50*, Routledge, London

HODDER, I. (1998) The interpretation of documents and material culture. In N.K. Denzin, Y.S. Lincoln (eds), *Collecting and Interpreting Qualitative Materials*, Sage, London, pp. 110–29

JAMES, E. (1951) *Education and Leadership*, Harrap, London

JONES, K. (2003) *Education in Britain: 1944 to the Present*, Polity, Cambridge

JUPP, V., NORRIS, C. (1993) Traditions in documentary analysis. In M. Hammersley (ed.), *Social Research: Philosophy, Politics and Practice*, Sage, London, pp. 37–51

KRAMNICK, I., SHEERMAN, B. (1993) *Harold Laski: A Life on the Left*, Hamish Hamilton, London

LABOUR PARTY CONFERENCE REPORT (1942), Labour Party, London

LATHAM, R., MATTHEWS, W. (eds) (1970) *The Diary of Samuel Pepys*, vol. I, 1660, G. Bell and Sons Ltd, London

LYND, R.S., LYND, H.M. (1929) *Middletown: A Study in American Culture*, Constable, London

McCULLOCH, G. (1982) Victor Gollancz on the crisis and prospects of Labour and the Left, 1942, *Bulletin of the Society for the Study of Labour History*, 44, pp. 18–22

McCULLOCH, G. (1988) From Currie to Picot: history, ideology and policy in New Zealand education, *Access*, 7, pp. 1–15

McCULLOCH, G. (1989) *The Secondary Technical School: A Usable Past?*, Falmer, London

McCULLOCH, G. (1990) Secondary school zoning: the case of Auckland. In J. Codd, R. Harker, R. Nash (eds), *Political Issues in New Zealand Education*, 2nd edn, Dunmore Press, Palmerston North, pp. 283–302

McCULLOCH, G. (1991a) School zoning, equity and freedom: the case of New Zealand, *Journal of Education Policy*, 6/2, pp. 155–68

McCULLOCH, G. (1991b) *Philosophers and Kings: Education for Leadership in Modern England*, Cambridge University Press, Cambridge

McCULLOCH, G. (1994) *Educational Reconstruction: The 1944 Education Act and the 21st Century*, Woburn, London

Bibliography

McCulloch, G. (1998) *Failing the Ordinary Child? The Theory and Practice of Working Class Secondary Education*, Open University Press, Buckingham

McCulloch, G. (2000a) Publicising the educational past. In D. Crook, R. Aldrich (eds), *History of Education for the 21st Century*, Institute of Education, London, pp. 1–16

McCulloch, G. (2000b) The politics of the secret garden: teachers and the school curriculum in England and Wales. In C. Day, A. Fernandez, T. Hauge, J. Moller (eds), *The Life and Work of Teachers: International Perspectives in Changing Times*, Falmer, London, pp. 26–37

McCulloch, G., Helsby, G., Knight, P. (2000) *The Politics of Professionalism: Teachers and the Curriculum*, Continuum, London

McCulloch, G., Richardson, W. (2000) *Historical Research in Educational Settings*, Open University Press, Buckingham

Major, J. (2000) *The Autobiography*, HarperCollins, London

Mangan, J.A. (1981/1986) *Athleticism in the Victorian and Edwardian Public School: The Emergence and Consolidation of an Educational Ideology*, Falmer, London

Marsden, W.E. (2001) *The School Textbook: Geography, History, and Social Studies*, Woburn, London

Marwick, A. (1965) *The Deluge: British Society and the First World War*, Macmillan, London

Marwick, A. (1968) *Britain in the Century of Total War: War, Peace and Social Change, 1900–1967*, Macmillan, London

Marwick, A. (1970) *The Nature of History*, Macmillan, London

Marwick, A. (1981) *The Nature of History*, 2nd edn, Macmillan, London

Marwick, A. (2001) *The New Nature of History: Knowledge, Evidence, Language*, Palgrave, London

May, T. (2001) *Social Research: Issues, Methods and Process*, 3rd edn, Open University Press, Buckingham

Mills, C. Wright (1959) *The Sociological Imagination*, Oxford University Press, London

Ministry of Education (1959) *15 to 18* (Crowther Report), HMSO, London

Ministry of Education (1963a) *Half Our Future* (Newsom Report), HMSO, London

Ministry of Education (1963b) *Higher Education* (Robbins Report), HMSO, London

Morgan, J. (ed.) (1981) *The Backbench Diaries of Richard Crossman*, Hamish Hamilton and Jonathan Cape, London

Morton, A. (1997) *Education and the State from 1833*, PRO Publications, London

Namier, L. (1960) *The Structure of Politics at the Accession of George III*, 2nd edn, Macmillan, London

New Zealand Department of Education (1944) *The Post-Primary School Curriculum* (Thomas Report), Government Printer, Wellington

New Zealand Department of Education (1962) *Report of the Commission on Education in New Zealand* (Currie Report), Government Printer, Wellington

Nora, P. (1996) General introduction: between memory and history. In P. Nora (ed.), *Realms of Memory*, vol. I: *Conflicts and Divisions*, Columbia University Press, New York, pp. 1–20

OBSERVER, THE (2002) Experts find fault with new 1901 census website, 6 January, p. 12

OGG, D. (1947) *Herbert Fisher 1865–1940: A Short Biography*, Edward Arnold and Co., London

OPENSHAW, R. (1995) *Unresolved Struggle: Consensus and Conflict in State Post-Primary Education*, Dunmore Press, Palmerston North

OXFORD ENGLISH DICTIONARY (1989), 2nd edn, Clarendon Press, Oxford

PASCAL, R. (1960) *Design and Truth in Autobiography*, Routledge and Kegan Paul, London

PETERS, M., MARSHALL, J. (1988) The politics of 'choice' and 'community', *Access*, 7, pp. 84–106

PETERSON, L. (1999) *Traditions of Women's Autobiography: The Poetics and Politics of Life Writing*, University Press of Virginia, London

PIMLOTT, B. (ed.) (1986a) *The Second World War Diary of Hugh Dalton, 1940–45*, Jonathan Cape, London

PIMLOTT, B. (ed.) (1986b) *The Political Diary of Hugh Dalton, 1918–40, 1945–60*, Jonathan Cape, London

PLATT, J. (1981) Evidence and proof in documentary research, *Sociological Review*, 29/1, pp. 31–66

PLATT, J. (1996) *A History of Sociological Research Methods in America, 1920–1960*, Cambridge University Press, Cambridge

PLUMMER, K. (2001) *Documents of Life 2: An Invitation to a Critical Humanism*, Sage, London

PONSONBY, A. (1923) *English Diaries: A Review of English Diaries from the Sixteenth to the Twentieth Century with an Introduction on Diary Writing*, Methuen, London

PONSONBY, A. (1933) *John Evelyn*, Heinemann, London

POTTS, A. (2000) Academic occupations and institutional change: reflections on researching academic life, *Academic Life and Work*, 1, pp. 369–403

PRIOR, L. (2003) *Using Documents in Social Research*, Sage, London

PUNCH, K. (1998) *Introduction to Social Research: Quantitative and Qualitative Approaches*, Sage, London

PURVIS, J. (1985) Reflections upon doing historical documentary research from a feminist perspective. In R. Burgess (ed.), *Strategies of Educational Research: Qualitative Methods*, Falmer, London, pp. 179–205

RANKE, F. (1970) The ideal of universal history. In F. Stern (ed.), *The Varieties of History from Voltaire to the Present*, 2nd edn, Macmillan, London, pp. 54–62

RICHARDS, J. (1988) *Happiest Days: The Public Schools in English Fiction*, Manchester University Press, Manchester

ROCKWELL, J. (1974) *Fact in Fiction: The Use of Literature in the Systematic Study of Society*, Routledge and Kegan Paul, London

ROSEN, H. (1998) *Speaking from Memory: The Study of Autobiographical Discourse*, Trentham Books, London

SARAN, R. (1985) The use of archives and interviews in research on education policy. In R. Burgess (ed.), *Strategies of Educational Research: Qualitative Methods*, Falmer, London, pp. 207–41

SCHAMA, S. (1999) People's history, *The Guardian*, 13 November, p. 24

Bibliography

SCOTT, D. (2000) *Reading Educational Research and Policy*, RoutledgeFalmer, London

SCOTT, J. (1990) *A Matter of Record: Documentary Sources in Social Research*, Polity, Cambridge

SECORD, J. (2000) *Victorian Sensation: The Extraordinary Publication, Reception, and Secret Authorship of Vestiges of the Natural History of Creation*, University of Chicago Press, Chicago

SELF, R.C. (ed.) (1995) *The Austen Chamberlain Diary Letters: The Correspondence of Sir Austen Chamberlain with His Sisters Hilda and Ida, 1916–1937*, Cambridge University Press/Royal Historical Society, Cambridge

SILVERMAN, D. (2000) *Doing Qualitative Research: A Practical Handbook*, Sage, London

SILVERMAN, D. (2001) *Interpreting Qualitative Data: Methods for Analysing Talk, Text and Interaction*, 2nd edn, Sage, London

SIMON, B. (2000) *A Life in Education*, Lawrence and Wishart, London

SINCLAIR, K. (1976) *Walter Nash*, Auckland University Press, Auckland

SMITH, B.G. (1998) *The Gender of History: Men, Women, and Historical Practice*, Harvard University Press, Cambridge, MA

SMITH, L.M., DWYER, D.C., PRUNTY, J.J., KLEINE, P.F. (1988) *Innovation and Change in Schooling: History, Politics, and Agency*, Falmer, London

SOCIOLOGY (1993) Editorial introduction, special issue on Biography and autobiography in sociology, 27/1, pp. 1–4

SPOLTON, L. (1962–3) The secondary school in post-war fiction, *British Journal of Educational Studies*, 9, pp. 125–41

STEEDMAN, C. (1999) The space of memory: in an archive, *History of the Human Sciences*, 11/4, pp. 65–83

STEEDMAN, C. (2001) *Dust*, Manchester University Press, Manchester

STOREY, R. (1978) The development of the Modern Records Centre, University of Warwick, *Archives*, 59, pp. 137–42

STRAY, C. (1994) Paradigms regained: towards a historical sociology of the textbook, *Journal of Curriculum Studies*, 26/1, pp. 1–29

SUTHERLAND, G. (1981) A view of education records in the nineteenth and twentieth centuries, *Archives*, 66, pp. 79–85

TASKFORCE TO REVIEW EDUCATION ADMINISTRATION (1988) *Administering for Excellence: Effective Administration in Education*, Government Printer, Wellington

TAYLOR, A.J.P. (ed.) (1971) *Lloyd George: A Diary by Frances Stevenson*, Hutchinson, London

TAYLOR, A.J.P. (ed.) (1975) *My Darling Pussy: The Letters of Lloyd George and Frances Stevenson 1913–41*, Weidenfeld and Nicolson, London

TAYLOR, S., BOGDAN, R. (1998) *Introduction to Qualitative Research Methods: A Guidebook and Resource*, 3rd edn, John Wiley, New York

THATCHER, M. (1995) *The Path to Power*, HarperCollins, London

THOMAS, W.I., ZNANIECKI, F. (1918–20/1927) *The Polish Peasant in Europe and America*, Dover Publications, New York (first published in five volumes; second edition, 1927, in two volumes; the references here are to the second edition)

TOMALIN, C. (2003) *Samuel Pepys: The Unequalled Self*, Viking, London

Tosh, J. (2002) *The Pursuit of History: Aims, Methods and New Directions in the Study of Modern History*, revised 3rd edn, Longman, London

Townend, D.M.R. (2000) How does substantive law currently regulate social science research? In D. Burton (ed.), *Research Training for Social Scientists*, Sage, London, pp. 109–33

Tyacke, S. (2001) Archives in a wider world: the culture and politics of archives, *Archivaria*, 52, pp. 1–25

Tyerman, C. (2000) *A History of Harrow School*, Oxford University Press, London

Velody, I. (1998) The archive and the human sciences: notes towards a theory of the archive, *History of the Human Sciences*, 11/4, pp. 1–16

Vincent, D. (1981) *Bread, Knowledge and Freedom: A Study of Nineteenth-Century Working Class Autobiography*, Methuen, London

Walford, G. (2001) *Doing Qualitative Educational Research: A Personal Guide to the Research Process*, Continuum, London

Waller, W. (1932/1967) *The Sociology of Teaching*, John Wiley and Sons, London

Warburton, T., Saunders, M. (1996) Representing teachers' professional culture through cartoons, *British Journal of Educational Studies*, 44/3, pp. 307–25

Warner, W.L., Lunt, P.S. (1941) *The Social Life of a Modern Community*, Yale University Press, New Haven, CT

Watt, I. (1957) *The Rise of the Novel: Studies in Defoe, Richardson and Fielding*, Chatto and Windus, London

Webb, E.J., Campbell, D., Schwartz, R., Sechrest, L. (1966) *Unobtrusive Measures: Nonreactive Research in the Social Sciences*, Rand McNally, London

Webb, S., Webb, B. (1932) *Methods of Social Study*, Longmans, Green and Co., London

Whyman, S. (1999) 'Paper visits': the post-Restoration letter as seen through the Verney family archive. In R. Earle (ed.), *Epistolary Selves*, Ashgate, Aldershot, pp. 15–36

Whyte, W.F. (1943/1981) *Street Corner Society: The Social Structure of an Italian Slum*, 3rd edn, University of Chicago Press, London

Young, H. (1991) *One of Us: A Biography of Margaret Thatcher*, 2nd revised edition, Pan, London

Young, M. (1958) *The Rise of the Meritocracy, 1870–2033: An Essay on Education and Equality*, Thames and Hudson, London

Young, R. (1981) Post-structuralism: an introduction. In R. Young (ed.), *Untying the Text: A Post-Structuralist Reader*, Routledge and Kegan Paul, London, pp. 1–28

Index

Lightning Source UK Ltd.
Milton Keynes UK
UKOW03f2247220114

225107UK00003B/13/P